Shadow of the Mountain

Preface and Acknowledgements

Not meant as a concise and chronological history of the Arkansas River Valley, the Shadow of the Mountain provides a snapshot of lives lived during the time period running from settlement in the early 1800's through the twentieth century. The focus of study is the region and people of the River Valley most familiar to the author.

Many of the stories are those passed down for generations by family, often completed by through historical research and documentation of county, state, and national data including military, marriage, church, and census data. In many instances, stories of individuals, personnel events, and even old letters and diaries are used to flesh out historical events. Much time and effort has been expended to provide as historical a perspective as possible of the events described.

In events involving the author and the people within the communities described, the events are collective memories of those involved and, like most Scotch-Irish story tellers, some degree of poetic license is expected and utilized. Permission of family members was granted for stories involving various individuals; in fact, without the assistance, old letters, photos, and family histories, much of this history would not be available and would be lost for future generations. In some instances where it was felt appropriate, names were excluded from the document.

It is never possible to include everything or every individual. More stories are left out than included and the author is constantly obtaining documents and insight into history that needs recorded before it is lost. Special thanks to the Trusty, Horn, Scrudder, Daniel, Moore, Johns, Hice, White, Rogers, Hatcher, Parsons, and Titsworth families for providing me information and stories.

A few of the stories are from my own experiences and life. The people I describe enriched my, and others, life with their humor, their moral character, and their zest for life. I hope you do not mind my sharing of those experiences with others. A special thanks to Jerald Rice, Marlene Moore, Joyce Friddle, Sonya Fletcher, and others for photos and historical information Our history is a book constantly being written and we leave it to others and future generations to tell that story.

This book is dedicated to the people who wrote and are writing my lives story; My Family!

Dana Nixon Varnell

Curtis H. Varnell Family, Christmas '14

The River Valley

The sun rises higher in the sky, pushing aside the darkness in the deep valleys and hollows that parallel its flight. Blue water bisects the region, flowing freely before being gathered as lakes behind tremendous man-made dams. Smaller tendrils of streams feed into the river; Vache Grasse, Mulberry, Shoal, Petit Jean and other creeks and streams feeding the serpentine waterway that course downstream to the colossal Mississippi river.

Flat-topped mountains, huge rounded domes and hogback ridges interspersed with pine and hardwood trees dot the landscape. Plains covered with deep, dark, rich, alluvial soils border the rivers and streams. Prior to the arrival of farmers, this region was covered by shallow pools of water, thickets, and huge cane breaks. Wildlife, especially deer and black bear, were found in abundance and small herds of woodland bison feed rich grasses.

Keel Boat

The River Valley is about one-hundred miles long and varies from a few to nearly forty miles wide. Today, it encompasses a region from Little Rock in the east to Fort Smith in the west and forms a division between the Ozark and the Ouachita Mountains. The earlies known white explorer was Hernando De Soto. De Soto arrived on the west coast of Florida on May 30, 1539 with 10 ships carrying over 600 soldiers, priests, and explorers. They spent four years searching for gold and silver, exploring the area, and brutally contacting native societies, including the Cherokees, Seminoles, Creeks, Appalachians, and Choctaws. During the expedition, he traveled up the Arkansas River, perhaps as far west as Fort Smith and possibly investigated Magazine and other local mountains. Archeology reports indicate Spanish armor, helmets, and other iron implements have been discovered in the River Valley. A mound-burial near Caulksville is reported to contain large men with armor as well as numerous natives. De Soto died during the explorations and was buried on the banks of the Mississippi River in late June, 1542. One of the lasting influences of his expedition was the eradication of much of the native population due to diseases carried by the explorers and for which the natives had no immunity. Very few natives were found in the area when the first white man settled in the early 1800's.

Prior to American settlers, French traders had journeyed to the area and established trade with natives. Buffalo robes, beaver, and other skin were traded for powder, ball, and trinkets. Buffalo, deer meat, corn, and other food were also traded and made its way to market in New Orleans. Vache Grasse Creek, Fourche LaFave River, and even the town of Lavaca owe their name to these early traders

The region became part of the United States with the Louisiana Purchase in 1803. Initially, a large portion of the River Valley was dedicated as Indian reservation and given to the Cherokee, Delaware, Choctaw, and other eastern tribes. Cherokee settled and built farms along the river from Russellville to Fort Smith. One of the earliest settlements was Dwight Mission, formed by missionaries to educate the natives. Sequoyah, the inventor of the Cherokee alphabet, lived near there for a period of time.

Delaware, Arkansas is named for the tribe settling in that community and Indian place names are common throughout the area. Eventually, the Arkansas part of Indian Territory was traded for areas to the west and the Cherokee were forced to move into Oklahoma.

Shortly after 1800, a few American settlers began to move into the region. When Fort Smith was established in 1817, the troops travelling up river mentioned a family by the name of Billingsley who owned a cabin and small farm on the Mulberry River. Later, this family moved to the mouth of Shoal Creek and set up residence in that area. Right across the river at Spadra, an Indian trading post served as a local mercantile and center for fur traders.

Early descriptions of Arkansas settlers, including those of naturalist Thomas Nuttal and author

1824 Dwight Mission

Friedrich Gerstacker, recognized the potential Arkansas contained but painted an image of its population as hardy, backward, uneducated people; an image which still persists.

Immigrants settling in Arkansas often used the Arkansas River as means of transport. Leaving the Mississippi, they pushed keel boats upstream and settled on prime farm land. By 1807, those traveling by land left Memphis or Helena and followed an overland path to Clarendon, Cadron (Conway), Morrilton, Dwight Mission, and then to Ft. Smith.

The New Madrid earthquake of 1812-13 disrupted much overland travel and it, along with the Civil War, was probably the two most devastating events in the history of the state. The forty mile long Lake St. Francis was formed when parts of the St. Francis River was diverted by the earthquake. The delta region became a quagmire of backwater, swamp, and black gumbo mud. Land travel became almost impossible. Even in 1834, a group of Creek men on the way to Oklahoma with livestock during the Trail of Tears found that it took two weeks to travel the distance from Memphis to Little Rock through the morass. Without the earthquake, the Archway to the West found in St. Louis might well be found in Fort Smith, the natural jumping off place for the forty-niners during the gold rush, except for the impassable east Arkansas swamp.

PORTRAIT OF MUREL.
Taken in the Tennessee State Prison at Nashville

Some of the earliest stories from the region revolved around the outlaw John A. Murrell. Murrell was known as the "The Reverend Devil." Murrell was born in 1806 to a Methodist minister and to a wife of "ill repute." He once stated that his father was a good, honest man but he thought no less of him because of it. His mother, a never do well, ran a tavern and taught he and his family to steal anything of value. She took anything they stole of value for herself, daring her minister husband to discipline either she or the children.

By his early teens, he had been captured while trying to steal a horse and had H.T. branded on his hand as a horse thief.

John, at an early age, organized a gang called the clan. He would pretend to preach and send his clan out to rob the congregations home while they were at church.

By the age of sixteen, he had ran away from home and travelled from place to place stealing, drinking, and carousing. He loved fashionable clothes, beautiful horses, and women- not necessarily in that order. Extremely brutal, his motto was, "Dead men tell no tales." He once killed a Texan for the grand sum of one dollar and fifty cents. He would sometimes rob his victims, remove the entrails, fill the cavity with rocks, and sink the body into the river. Mark Twain describes some of Murrell's atrocities in his book, *Life on the Mississippi* and indicates that Murrell eventually had nearly one-thousand men in his clan. One of Murrell's most ambitious plans was to start a slave uprising and take over the city of New Orleans. Murrell travelled the byways and up and down the Mississippi and its tributaries. He was especially fond of caves and was said to stash the money he had accumulated in those caves. There are many stories of his travels. He carved his initials in a tree in eastern Arkansas- a fact which lead to the town's name of Marked Tree. Traveling up the Arkansas River, it is rumored that he debarked near the ferry in Roseville and that he and his men spent several days hid out in the hills. Tanyard Mountain, in close proximity to Roseville, would have been the logical site for Murrell to hide out but it was occupied by the Titsworth's and other families. As a hideout, Horseshoe or Short Mountain would better serve the purpose. Both are riddled with caves and openings, both have flat, smooth tops that allow views in all directions, and both, though close to the river, were very isolated in the 1830's. Where exactly did they camp? Did Murrell hid wealth in the caves? Many questions are left unanswered.

Murrell was captured in Tennessee in 1834. He spun many tales of his atrocities and hidden treasures while in prison before dying in 1844. It is reported that two doctors dug up his body, decapitated it and took the head to examine to determine what could make a man so evil.

As eastern states became more populated and land more expensive, settlers began to explore the new lands acquired through the Louisiana Purchase. Many of these men, given land grants as reward for fighting in the War of 1812, were looking for extensive acreage of rich farm lands where they could raise cotton. The flood plain of the Arkansas River and its tributaries afforded promising land for settlement.

By the 1820's, a group of businessmen including John Drennen, had established Van Buren as a trading post and steamboat landing. In 1819, a group of explorers passing up-river from Little Rock, loosened an arrow at the big arc of the river with the expectation of developing a town on the site where the arrow landed. The town was Ozark and the exact

John "Jack" Titsworth

site where the arrow landed, the Franklin County Courthouse.

Before 1821, Jack Titsworth signed a treaty with the Choctaw Indians and acquired land in what is now Logan County. He married Adalissa Clark and established a very prosperous plantation along the river. He and other planters established the steamboat port of Roseville, regarded as a substantial city in that period of time.

Steamboats plied up and down the Arkansas River by the late 1820's with cotton and other goods shipped to market in New Orleans and elsewhere.

When the river was low, goods coming upriver were offloaded at Dardanelle, Clarksville, or Roseville and delivered up the Military Road to Fort Smith and beyond.

Many famous individuals traversed the region, including John Audubon, Washington Irving, Wyatt Earp, President Zachary Taylor, Davy Crockett, James Bowie, Sam Houston, and others. During the administration of President Andrew Jackson, tribes from the southeastern portion of the United States were forcibly removed from their lands and settled in Indian Territory. The Western Cherokee, those that settled along the Arkansas River in the early 1800's, had already traded their lands locate in Arkansas for territory near present day Tahlequah. Other groups, including the Creek, Seminole, Choctaw, and Eastern Cherokee were forced out of their native lands and resettled. Many of these "civilized" tribes lived much like the white settlers. They dressed in western style clothing, lived in homes, and farmed the land. Some had adopted plantation cultivation and owned slaves. Regardless, the natives were gathered in large groups and, accompanied by U.S. troops, forced to the west. Referred to as the Trail of Tears, there was no one pathway to Indian Territory. Many of the routes involved both travel by boat and land. Often, the civilized Indian owned extensive property including large amounts of livestock.

When this situation occurred, women and children would travel by boat while the men trailed along on land with the animals.

Regardless of route or method, the trip was hard and hazardous. Many of the tribes were forced to travel in the harshest weather conditions and when coupled with poor food rations and sanitation, resulted in tremendous loss of life.

From 1828 to nearly 1840, many of these groups voyaged by boat to Dardanelle or Roseville and traveled overland up the Old Military Road or along what is now highway 64 to Fort Smith and into Indian Territory.

One such journey is described in the journal kept of Lieutenant Edward Deas who escorted a group of Cherokee westward during April of 1838. The group left Little Rock on a steamboat by that name. The steamboat pulled two heavily loaded keel boats containing possessions owned by the Indian. The larger of the keel boats continually ran aground. Deas, alarmed by the smallpox that plagued the local population and fearful that delay might cause it to spread to the Indians, left the larger keel boat behind. Shallow water forced the steamboat to place passengers on shore where they were forced to walk along the bank until deeper water was reached. A difficult task today, walking through the cane and brush of 1830's Arkansas would have been an arduous task. The group arrived in Roseville on the steamboat Little Rock on April 20, 1838. Unable to proceed further by boat, the group was offloaded at Titsworth's landing and spent four days obtaining wagons and mules to continue the journey. Obtaining seventeen wagons, the group proceeded south to the Old Military road and then through Grand Prairie.

Deas mentions in passing that two sickly children, one a slave, died overnight while the group camped on Vache Grasse creek near present day Lavaca.

On April 28, the group arrived at Fort Smith and proceeded across the river by ferry, entering Indian Territory by nightfall. The diary, a military report, succinctly discusses the condition of the road, the time required to travel, and even the expense engendered. Little is mentioned of the hardships and human suffering on the Trail of Tears.

Arkansas and the River Valley grew rapidly during the 1840's and 1850's. By 1836, Arkansas

Lakeport Plantation, Lake Village, AR.

population was large enough to reach statehood and it entered the Union at the same time as Michigan. Arkansas more than doubled its population each ten year census from 1830 to 1850. Hugh numbers of settlers entered Arkansas from Tennessee and surrounding states.

The southern and eastern portion of the state, along with the rich bottom lands of Arkansas became cotton country. Steamboats plied up and down the rivers, loading bales of cotton to be shipped north or to Great Britain. Most of the large plantations were ran by individuals of English descent, a very distinct group from the Scotch-Irish that settled the upland areas and lived on small farm.

In addition, one-fourth of the population was brought into the state as

Paris Family working cotton in the bottoms in the 1930's

slaves and forced into involuntary servitude clearing and planting the cotton crops. Most of these individuals were also found in large plantations in the delta. The hardiest and most capable of the slaves were used to clear and drain the swamps

Cotton steam-boat in Camden, AR

10

of southeast Arkansas. These swamplands, many created by the New Madrid earthquake, were quagmires and required backbreaking labor under the most inhospitable circumstances to develop. For the slaves, life and existence could be brutal.

By 1860, great fissures existed within the economic, social, and cultural groups found in the state. These fissures were to result in the most traumatic and demanding period of Arkansas history and no place were the fissures more evident than within the Arkansas River valley.

**Scranton Bank
1912**

1912 Scranton Bank on a busy day

Scott County Civil War Memorial

Cowie Winery

12

The Uncivil War

By the time the Civil War began, several thousand people lived in the area that would become Logan County. The largest towns, if you could call them that, included Roseville, Shoal Creek, Revellie, Chismville, and Booneville. Better described as villages, these communities generally consisted of a post office, blacksmith shop, grist mill, and hardware store. Some, like Roseville, would have merchants that traded products that were brought up-river by steamboat and have offices for those wishing to ship products to the bigger markets in New Orleans, Memphis, or St. Louis. When water levels were high enough, steamboats made regular delivery to the docks at Spadra and Roseville. During low water cycles, goods were delivered to Dardanelle and were off-loaded to wagon for delivery.

Old Military Road at Short Mountain Creek

The Military Road from Fort Gipson to Memphis was completed in 1836. The road ran north of the river to Dardanelle, crossed the river by ferry at that point, and then proceeded to Fort Smith along a route that parallels what is now highway 22. Roads also ran from Russelville to Clarksville and from there to Van Buren. Those wishing to do so could cross the Arkansas River from Spadra to Morrison Bluff by ferry. A road ran from there south, crossed the Military Road and continued through St. Louis Valley, Red Bench, Revellie, and Chismville. To the south of Magazine Mountain, another major road connected Little Rock, Perryville, and Booneville with north south connections that lead to Hot Springs. Other, smaller roads were connected to these, many not much more than mere trails.

In 1860, life in much of Arkansas more closely resembled *Ole Yeller* than *Gone with the Wind*. It is true that there were some majestic plantations in the state, even a few in the Arkansas River Valley, but most lived a much simpler existence of sustenance farming. The farmers raised vegetables, livestock and a money crop of corn or cotton on small farms.

According to census data from 1860, 70% of the population of Arkansas consisted of these small yeoman farmers who, on average, owned no slaves, 80 acres of land, two or three cattle, and a horse. Most of the necessities and food came from the land. Livestock, especially pork, was abundant with a grown pig selling for $3.50. Like most southerners at the time, Arkansan's ate an average of about one-hundred and fifty pounds of pork per person. Greasy Valley, located just south of Paris, was supposedly given its name from the amount of lard rendered and sold by its citizens. Corn, which was produced in abundance throughout the state, provided the staple for survival.

Many of the homes were of European style with a single story, gable-roofed building of wood-frame or log consisting of one room with a single chimney placed along one wall. The more fortunate and most common consisted of two of these rooms connected with a common roof, separated by a dog-trot. The reconstructed Logan House at Chismville is a great example of this type of home. Surrounding outbuildings

Restored Dogtrot Home, Chismville, AR.

included a privy, chicken house, barn, and a root cellar. Water was obtained from a spring, running stream, or dug well.

Most of the people were religious in nature; products of the Great Awakening that occurred throughout the western states in the early 1800's. Methodist brought southern evangelism into Arkansas; they were soon joined by Cumberland Presbyterian, Baptists, and others that preached gospel by circuit riding through the isolated communities. These denominations especially appealed to the Scotch-Irish immigrants found in the mountains of the Ozarks and Ouachita's. Many of the immigrants lived in communities of people that had migrated into the area together. The area just north of Magazine Mountain attracted a large number of families from Hamilton County, Tennessee. These included the Scrudder, Trusty, Horn, Rhineheart, Parson, and Varnell's. Arkansas offered fresh start, new land, at low prices to settlers so perhaps one family would migrate and then entice others to move. Residents of Hamilton County also may have moved due to land title problems as a result of the State of Franklin incident. During the early 1800's, as unsettled lands obtained population, the citizens could apply to become a territory and then a state. The people in what is now eastern Tennessee filed to become the state of Franklin; when that did not happen, the land titles and ownership may have been jeopardized and contributed to the willingness of people to move. Land in Arkansas was offered at very reasonable rates and, to veterans of the War of 1812, as rewards for service. For various reasons, many of the residents from Logan County originated from Alabama, Georgia, and Tennessee.

By 1860, Arkansas was emerging as a prosperous and industrious state. Land was still available and cheap, the climate was warm and welcoming, and there was a variety of opportunities for people moving into the area. The major discord within the state concerned slavery. Much of the prosperity of Arkansas was based on the growth of cotton, a sixteen million dollar industry in the state. More than 111,000 slaves toiled the land to produce this cotton- with large concentrations

15

of these cotton producing plantations and slaves (74%) located in the delta or in the bottomlands along major rivers.

With the election of Abraham Lincoln, the wealthy land owners' way of life was threatened. Those regions of Arkansas having large slave populations had no problem in aligning themselves with the more radical states such as South Carolina that were demanding to be allowed to succeed from the Union.

Merchants and the small farmers scattered through the highland area of the state were more divided in opinion. Most families in the mountainous areas owned no slaves (only one in five families in the entire state owned slaves) and many had personnel objections to their ownership. Many of these were strong Unionist and would never support secession. Others were upset over the idea of state rights- the right of a state to have powers to govern themselves and make their own decisions- and were willing to leave the Union over that issue.

Lakeport Plantation near Lake Village,

T. DeBlack, ATU

The Arkansas River Valley is about seventy-five miles long and varies in width from twelve to twenty-five miles or so. Lands along the Arkansas River and some of its tributaries are quite rich and productive. McClain Bottoms produced some of the best cotton crops in the state and Roseville served as one of the busiest ports along the river. Other shipping areas existed at Patterson Bluff, Spadra, and Dardanelle. Several plantation type farms existed in those areas and large numbers of slaves were owned by some of the farmers. Highland cotton, not nearly as large or productive, was grown by people along the streams and ridges of the Magazine Mountain range. Most of these farmers raised other crops for sustenance and cotton as a money crop. This cotton was generally grown by the family but some of the farmers owned a few slaves. Hardy Banks of Magazine Township in Yell County provides an example of these small slave owners. He was a subsistence farmer cultivating various crops including cotton, grew some livestock, and also produced oak binders used on cotton bales. He had four slaves; a man, woman, and two children. These slaves were involved with all these activities, working side by side with Mr. Banks and his family. They lived in an adjacent dog-trot cabin and often hunted together. Even though this sounds less harsh, and probably was, than life from *Uncle Tom's Cabin*, it was less than idyllic. Slaves were property and could be bought, sold, and families divided up at the whim of the owner. Owners relied heavily on punishment, especially whipping, as a form of keeping slaves in "line."

What is now Logan County was located in Johnson and Franklin County, Arkansas until 1873. The 1850 census data shows that Johnson County had a population of 5,227 free and 731 slaves. Franklin County had a similar distribution with 3,972 free and 473 slaves. Most of the slaves in Franklin County were in the hands of a few wealthy landowners located in Short Mountain and Six Mile Township. John Titsworth and his heirs alone owned 216 of these slaves.

There were eight Johnson County townships is 1850. Clark Township (Patterson Bluff and part of McClain Bottoms) had the highest slave population; close to one-fourth of the population. Perry Township (Lamar) and Horsehead Township, both containing rich bottom land, had similar ratios. Mulberry and Piney Townships, located in the mountainous regions, had virtually no slave population. From this data, one can deduct that people living along the river had the majority of the slaves and the most reason to support the Confederacy. Cities such as Roseville and Clarksville also had a proportionally large slave population- labor to run the gins, load the steam-boats, and assist in shipping cotton.

Traveling through McClain bottoms in 1860, one would have observed vast cotton fields being plowed, planted, or harvested by slave labor. Slave life rotated around the plantation system. During the winter months, land was cleared of scrub brush and trees. In February, the fields would be plowed by horse and mule team and prepared for early planting which would take place in April and May. By June, the cotton plants were up and hoeing to clear fields of weeds took up most of the slave's time. This backbreaking work continued throughout the summer. September and November was spent picking the cotton and taking it to the gin to be processed. The cotton gin, developed by Eli Whitney in the late 1700's, was in wide-use and several were located in the River Valley. Once processed, the cotton was stored to be shipped to New Orleans via the many steam boats that plied the waters of the Arkansas River. Smaller keel boats were used to deliver cotton down the smaller Petit Jean and Fouche Rivers.

The Titsworth family of Roseville were typical of the "Old South" plantation system. The original plantation was established by Colonel Issac Titsworth in the early 1800's. Isaac Titsworth was born on October 14, 1749 in Bridgewater, New Jersey. He was an American patriot and served from 1174-1776 in the Continental Army. After the war, he sought his fortune by moving first to North Carolina and thus to Kentucky. Reasons for his movement is not known but certainly included the opportunity to obtain land at very cheap prices. As a war veteran and hero, no doubt he received some of his pay as land grants.

Isaac kept a diary of his travels and adventures. While migrating westward with his and his brother John's family, they were attacked by Creek Indians near Red River, Tennessee. The incident occurred on October 5, 1794 at about midnight. Isaac rounded up his children and tried to hide his children. He and his wife returned fire on the Indian. Their daughter Peggy refused to be separated and was trying to assist with reloading the weapons. The Creek attack overran the group. One of the men was about to tomahawk Peggy when Isaac's wife threw herself between daughter and attacker. The tomahawk split her forehead and killed her instantly. Thirteen year old Margaret was captured along with two other of Isaac's children. The Creeks also killed John Titsworth, his wife, one of his children, and captured one of John's slaves. Major Maulden, of the local forces, pursued the Creek the next day. When pressed, the Indian killed another of Issac's children and wounded and scalped another of John Titsworth's children. The boy survived but was badly scarred by the incident. The other children, except Margaret, were killed during the militia pursuit.

Isaac placed a reward notice in all newspapers in the region, offering a reward for the return of his family. Margaret remained in captivity for three years until Isaac, hearing of her whereabouts, negotiated with the Indians and obtained her release.

Isaac appears to be a man of the frontier, constantly selling his property and moving westward. He lived for a time in Kentucky, Southern Illinois, and along the Ohio River where he maintained a ferry. In 1813, he arrived at Short Mountain, Arkansas with a group of soldiers. Much of Arkansas was Indian Territory at that time and Cherokee had settled along prime sites north of the River. Isaac negotiated the purchase of property near Roseville and moved there with his family, eventually establishing a plantation and several businesses. He survived to old age, dying at age 83 in 1832. He was first buried on his property but his body was eventually exhumed and buried at Oakwood cemetery in Paris.

Isaac was married at least three times and produced a number of off-spring, several of whom survived to adulthood. John "Jack" Titsworth, born in 1802, was the son to carry on the family home and name in the River Valley.

Jack married Adalissa Quinn Clark on December 5, 1827. They had nine children, five of whom survived to adulthood. These included William C., John Randolph, Narcissa Ada, Almon, and

Edwin. William died at an early age of twenty-one so care of the property passed to Jack. The younger two Titsworth brothers never married.

The Titsworth holdings and estate included much of Roseville, McClain Bottoms, and extensive property ownership throughout present day Logan County. When the Civil War began, the Titsworths owned 213 slaves and were clearing land as far south as Wildcat Mountain road south of present day Paris.

Adalisa (Clark) Titsworth

In contrast to the individuals found in the rich farm lands of the Arkansas River floodplain, people living up on the benches and ridges were small yeoman farmers. Fiercely independent, most had no slaves and little reason to support the flat-landers who did. They scratched out a living on the rocky soils and perhaps raised a small amount of cotton as a cash crop. Some of these men supported the rights to own slaves; others were adamantly opposed to it. With the attack on Fort Sumter, South Carolina and the subsequent withdrawal of the Southern States from the Union, all of these individuals were faced with the biggest decision of their lives; to remain a part of the Union or to take up arms against their country.

The Civil War in Arkansas was a bitter affair that divided neighbors and families into warring factions. The bitterness and atrocities associated with war in the Middle East would be nothing new to many of those who survived the Uncivil War that occurred in the River Valley.

The United States has had a long tradition of training an armed militia that could be called upon during periods of need. Arkansas, and most states, required that young men, be trained to serve in the militia. Although not as strong as it had been following the War with Mexico in 1846, young men in towns across the state would meet and drill as militia that could be called upon by the government when needed. As sectional frictions began to heat up, more and more young men as well as veterans from prior service began to join these forces. By 1860 the state's militia consisted of 62 regiments divided into eight brigades, which comprised an eastern division and a western division. New regiments were added as the militia organization developed. Additionally, many counties and cities raised uniformed volunteer companies. These local groups developed their own uniforms, flags, and often bought their own equipment.

When the war began, these groups were called upon by the state to take up arms against the

Union. Units located in Little Rock and Fort Smith quickly seized the local military outposts and weapons for the Confederacy. In the rural areas, many of the more ardent supporters of the militia joined the regular Confederate forces.

Arkansas had 21,500 troops enter the war on the side of the South. That's half as many men as the state had voting in 1860. Fort Smith, with a population of 2,500, had five

Major General Thomas Hindman

21

hundred men sign up to fight for the Confederacy. Many River Valley residents, swayed by the patriotic speeches, fanfare, and the chance to escape the tedium of following the south end of a north bound mule, left the local militia and joined regular Confederate units that were being formed across the South. A few had the courage and fortitude to travel north and join Union forces in Missouri and other areas. Some of both groups of these Arkansan's fought at Wilson's Creek in Missouri and later in the loosing battles of Pea Ridge and Prairie Groove. As the war intensified and enlistment periods ended, several of these men term of enlistment ended and they returned home. A few, disenchanted with war or opposed to being shipped to the Eastern War Theater, simply deserted and returned home.

The 58th Regiment Arkansas Militia was part of the old prewar Arkansas State Militia organization, and constituted the militia unit for the area of southern Franklin County which is now in Logan County. Units within the 58th included the 7th militia, Franklin County with company captains including John Titsworth and Albert Moffit. The 10th militia unit was formed in Clarksville and included many men from south of the river. The more ardent individuals transferred to permanent Confederate units and many were transferred east of the Mississippi to fight. Other individuals were conscripted and forced to join the war; even though they secretly did not support the Southern cause. This was to have dramatic effect on the war effort in Northwest Arkansas.

Even with depleted ranks, the 58th continued to meet, drill, and march during 1861 and into the early months of 1862. No doubt many of these men were Northern sympathizers who wished to remain near their families but did not care to join the wider war effort. They mustered for annual inspection and drill during the period February 22 to March 21, 1862, probably at Roseville and Clarksville. By that time, Northwest Arkansas had been lost to the Confederacy and most of the men in permanent units had been shipped east. Many of the locals, signed up for limited terms in the militia, had already had their fill of the war. Many of these either deserted or, if their term of enlistment had ran out, simply laid down their arms and returned to their homes.

General Thomas Hindman was placed in charge of the Trans-Mississippi region which included much of Arkansas. Left without an army, he began to force conscription of all able-bodied men from across the state. This included all of the remainder of these militia units that were physically able to fight as well as those whose terms of service were over. Those left, primarily old men and boys who were otherwise disqualified from active service, became members of the Home Guard. This group was later commissioned to begin guerrilla operations against Union forces and Union sympathizers. General Hindman also began actively acquiring supplies and munitions by foraging supplies from the citizenry as well as authorizing groups of guerilla to carry out war against Union troops and sympathizers.

With forced conscription of all able-bodied men from sixteen to forty, men opposed to the confederacy had only two choices: flee North or hide-out. Neither choice was easy but to not do so left one open to attack from the home guard, guerilla units, or even neighbors. Those fleeing would have to pass through territory held by Southern troops as they journeyed making it nearly impossible to take their wives or families with them.

A large group of these men existed throughout the River Valley. Records seem to indicate that several of these men, especially those with military experience from the Mexican War, left early in the war and joined Federal units in Missouri. These included James Laferry of Ellsworth, James Garner, and several of their family members. Both were experienced soldiers and were welcome additions to Union forces. Because both North and South thought that the war would be over within a short time, most of these initial enlistments were for less than a year, leaving the men free to join other groups or units as the war progressed.

One group of men opposed to the war joined into a loose federal guerrilla unit called the "Mountain Feds." During 1861 and 1862, Confederate forces occupied all of the River Valley and made it very difficult for these men to survive. The loose bond that existed between them allowed for communication concerning the movement of home guard and Confederate troops that were moving through the area. Warned about the approach of these men, the "mountain Feds," would flee into the rocky cliffs and overhangs of Magazine, Short, and Rich Mountain. From the high elevations, they could observe any troops moving in the area and, because there were very few places to access the mountain tops, they could easily evade capture.

Sometimes it was not so easy on the family left behind. Neighbors would report people they thought were Union sympathizers to the authorities. The authorities then would retaliate against

William "Wild Bill" Heffington

the family by stealing their food and goods, burning their homes, threatening the families, and, in some case, of beating or killing family members. As the war progressed and more and more people lost family to the war effort, the atrocities on both sides became even more violent.

One of the more famous "Unionist" in the region was "Wild Bill Heffington." Heffington, the illegitimate son of Louisa McBride, was born in 1830 in Wayne, Tennessee. Louisa had four other children who went by the name of McBride before marrying Hugh Shott and settling in the area near Havana. She and Shott had five additional children together. Heffington married Elizabeth Tritt and, by 1850, had followed his mother to Arkansas and built a farm on

24

the southern flanks of Magazine Mountain. At that time, he was known as William McBride, but upon discovering his father's real name, legally changed his name to William Heffington. What little is known of Heffington indicates that he was a small yeoman farmer, had six children in a short span of years, and was widely respected around the community as a hunter and explorer. No doubt, he hunted and explored the wilderness of the surrounding mountains and knew many of the caves, crevasses, and hideouts that he put to good use during the war year.

When the war began, he either joined or was conscripted into Company F, 17th Arkansas Infantry, Confederate States of America (CSA) in December of 1861. Several men from Yell County were also in this unit, including Samuel and George Witt, William Shott, and members of the Owen's family. Heffington must have proven an able soldier and leader because he advanced quickly to the rank of Lieutenant.

The 17th Arkansas was a highly respected and decorated unit and participated in the Battle of Pea Ridge on March 7 and 8th of 1862. The commanding officer of the 17th was Lt. Col. John Griffith. Southern forces proved inept during the battle and many of the men were discouraged by actions taken by CSA General Van Dorn. During the battle on March 8th, the 17th was being hard-pressed by the Union and had little or no ammunition. A letter written after the war by Captain

Captain Benjamin Chism

Benjamin B. Chism, grandson of James Logan, explains the predicament faced by the 17th on the second day of the battle. The 17th had started to slowly retreat from the field when an artillery officer galloped up to Col. Griffith and said to him, "For God's sake, save my battery!" Three or four pieces of artillery were nearly surrounded by enemy cavalry. Col. Griffith answered, "General, I have no ammunition, but I can use the bayonet!" The command was given, "Regiment, fall into line, guard against the cavalry." Boone stated, "In this position we stood in line until the Federal Cavalry had flanked us pretty well on the left and rear, at this juncture a Missouri CSA Regiment passed near to us, making its way after our retreating army. When it was found the enemy was in or nearly in our rear, the command was given to move, and we started at a double quick, but we could not follow the army. My recollection is we moved North pursued by the Federal Cavalry. We were cut off from the main army and the pursuit of us by the enemies' cavalry continued till late in the evening. When traveling in the mountains, we returned to the army. At this time General Pike was seen making his way from the direction of the battlefield accompanied by two or three aids. He was hailed by Col. Griffith and asked what should be done." The men discovered that General Van Dorn had already retreated without them and they were ordered by General Pike to disband in groups of five or six men and to make their own way back to Van Buren.

What a way to fight a war!! More than half of the men never made it back to Van Buren, the ones that did were taken to East of the Mississippi along with Van Dorn to fight the rest of the in other states.

Heffington was reported as a deserter on May 20, 1862 and spent the rest of his life as an ardent opponent of the Confederacy. Several explanations could be offered for his change of heart. He may have been discouraged and upset at Van Dorn's leadership and the fact that he left Heffington's troops unaided. It was also a well-known fact that Confederate troops in Arkansas were ill provided and provisioned. Most of the supplies, horses, and weapons were sent east to the larger theaters of war. General Jo Shelby, criticized because his troops were dressed in confiscated blue union uniforms, remarked that his men had not been provided one uniform during the course of the war. In contrast, some of the Confederate officers were superbly dressed in dandy uniforms, hats topped with ostrich feathers, and accompanied onto the field with servants who waited on them hand and foot. Heffington did not appear to be a man that was intimidated by class status or rank or one that would particularly like to be exposed to Southern aristocracy. General Pike, who obviously was on the field with Heffington's men, was commander of forces from the Indian Nation. During the battle of Pea Ridge, his troops butchered and scalped Union troops. The explanation for Heffingtons desertion could well be the discouragement and disenchantment resulting from the conduct above, from lack of commitment, or that he simply did not wish to leave his wife and family. For whatever reason, he returned home and quickly joined the Union cause. In a twist of fate, after the war, his wife Elizabeth filed for and received a pension for him from the CSA.

Upon his return, Heffington wasted no time organizing guerilla forces committed to the Union cause. By late 1862, this group contained over one-hundred and twenty five men and was strong enough to retaliate against Confederate home guard and militia sent out to capture them. By this time, forces from both sides were carrying out every type of crime and depredation possible against each other. Confederate forces made life very difficult for those thought to be Union sympathizers. Often, Southern troops would appear at these peoples home and leave with all available food as well as with the family's cattle, horses, and pigs. Any child or adult of acceptable age would be forced to join Southern forces. Resistance on the part of the family would result in beatings, the home being burned to the ground, and sometimes other atrocities. James Taylor of Clarksville claimed Rebel bushwhackers attacked his home, robbed him of money, cattle, and horses and then, for good measure, decided to hang him. His brother happened upon the incident just as James was hung. He fired off his gun and the bushwhackers fled. Taylor's wife and kids were able to remove the rope before he choked to death.

Heffington and his group responded to such atrocities with a vengeance. Riding in groups across the region, they burned, pillaged, and robbed those that opposed them. It was during this period of time when Irben White grandfather was returning from a trip to Dardanelle with this father. The White Family lived in the Mt. Salem community on the north slope of Magazine Mountain. As they approached home, they noticed buzzards circling and landing near the road. As the boy and his father approached, buzzards flew into the air, exposing the body upon which they were feeding. The body was that of a local man who had been very vocal in his expression of support of the Confederacy and had probably been involved in actions against his neighbors. His body, what remained of it, was riddled by bullets. Free-roaming hogs had gotten to the body first, pulling pieces of it in all directions. Both of them were sickened by the sight-even more so when they realized that they had to inform the wife and family of his death.

Growing every braver, his group raided throughout the River valley. Heffington was viewed as a Robin Hood by the North, a worthless freebooter, thief, and criminal by the South. His forces were strong enough at one time that he is thought to have maintained a prison for Southern sympathizers near the present town day town of Belleville. He is said to have hung several men and, in at least one case, a woman who refused to supply him information he desired. He and his band terrorized the region and once sent the entire town of Dardanelle into a panic when he raided within three miles of Dardanelle port. Stories of his activities appeared in newspapers in Fort Smith and Little Rock. Alarmed, Southerners demanded that more forces be sent into the area to capture and punish the man now known as "Wild Bill." As Confederate forces moved into the area, "Wild Bill" fell back into the mountains for protection and as a defensive position.

The various grotto's, crevasses, and caves offered plenty of shelter for the men. Several small rock houses are found on Magazine, Huckaberry, and Rich Mountain and are thought to be secure places that Mountain Feds used to hide out. From the top plateau of the mountain, one can see for miles. Any large troop movements would be easily detected and avoided by Heffington and his men.

Rock House on Magazine

They could also detect movement of small supply trains moving back and forth from Fort Smith and Little Rock, rush down from their mountain hideaway, and set up places of ambush. A large group of Confederate Cavalry eventually trailed Heffington and his group of more than 125 raiders up the side of the mountain. A large skirmish involving possibly 250 or more men occurred at Snake Knob on the south side of Mt. Magazine. Heffington and his men were successful. Heffington was obtaining a reputation as a fearless fighter, a mountain man in the Natty Bumppo vein. Riding his horse and carrying his gun, "Old Silversides," he and his ragtag gang would appear near Dardanelle, the next at Fort Smith, and even up into the Boston Mountains.

By early 1863, Federal troops had occupied Fayetteville and controlled much of Northwest Arkansas. Heffington was finding it more and more difficult to maintain enough supplies, powder, and weapons to carry on the increasingly larger fight in the River Valley. In March of 1863, he and 146 men from the area forded the Arkansas River and made their way to Fayetteville where they joined the Union cause and were formed into the Arkansas First Infantry. Heffington was named Captain of a group that included George and Levi Fink, Henry and Edly

29

Rogers, William Shrewder (Scrudder?), Isaac Wiggins, and several of the White family. Most of this group came from Magazine and Chickalah Mountain.

In early 1863, Federal troops had moved into N.W. Arkansas and had control over most of the towns around Fayetteville. Like Heffington, other men sympathetic to the Union cause journeyed north to join up with the Union troops. At Fayetteville, it is likely that Heffington and his men ran across several like-minded men from the River Valley. James Garner of Reveillee and Captain James LaFerry of Ellsworth, friends and former colleagues during the Mexican War, were a part of the First Infantry as was a young Private William Parker. Parker, born in 1842, is thought to be the son of William S. Parker who had fought alongside of LaFerry and Garner in the Mexican War. Like Heffington, he had been conscripted and then deserted from the Confederate forces. All three of these men, plus many others from the First Infantry, would be instrumental in the war effort as well as the politics of Logan County.

No uniform, supplies, or barracks existed for these new recruits. The First Arkansas Cavalry were only in name as there were only a couple hundred horses for the nearly 900 men. The First Infantry were a rag-tag group

Tebbetts House, Union Headquarters

with no uniforms and only equipped with weapons that had been left on the field at Prairie Groove. Fortunately for them, these consisted of several of the new .58 caliber rifles with a range of 400 yards but several also had to be content with the old .69 caliber smoothbore.

On April 17, 1863, Confederate troops under General William Cabell and 900 troops moved up the road from Ozark and onto the ridge just east of Fayetteville. At daybreak, they opened fire on Union headquarter located in the Tebbetts House on Dickson Street. The cannon barrage proved ineffective as did fighting with field weapons. Even more poorly equipped than the First Infantry, many of the Confederates were armed with shotguns and ineffective swords and long knives. The Springfields, with a range of 400 yards, kept the Rebels at bay. Thinking that the Arkansas Cavalry would flee, General Caball ordered the Confederate cavalry to charge. A vicious battle along Arkansas Avenue ensued, often virtually hand to hand fighting. During this charge, William C. Parker and George Smith were in the thick of the battle cheering on their men. Both men were wounded in the head, though not seriously and both men were commended for their bravery.

The battle raged on until noon, the majority of the fighting located at the intersection of College Avenue and Dickson Street. Several buildings were burned to the ground during the fight. Eventually, Cabell's artillery ran out of ammunition and he was forced to withdraw from the battle and return to Ozark. An estimated 50 men were killed and several injured.

This could be regarded as a futile battle, as many in most wars are, because on April 25th, 1863, all the Union troops in Fayetteville were ordered to retreat to Missouri, leaving the town and its people again undefended by troops. Heffington was again left with a choice of accompanying the army or remaining near his home. Elizabeth was again pregnant. With three young children to feed and care for and with uncertain circumstances at home, Bill decided to return home. It is ironic that he now had enlisted and fought with both armies of the Civil War and still did not possess a uniform to show for it. On the way home and fearful of detection, he carefully wrapped his gun, Old Silversides, and placed it in a sheltered area. Possibly he took some of his men, including the ill George Fink, and supplies back to Magazine Mountain. Fink was the child of Levi Fink, who along with the Lipe's and Harkey's, had migrated to Harkey's

31

valley in 1846 from Cabarrus County, North Carolina. He probably subsisted with Harrington and the "Mountain Feds" until his chronic illness caused him to give out. He had a large family in the area and, very likely, Harrington left him with his sister Elizabeth who was married to Moses Harkey. Yell County historical society states that on or about September 20, 1863, he was captured near his home by Confederate guerrillas. He and his sister Elizabeth were hung. Harrington would not have been able to stay with his wife and family. For his safety and theirs, he stayed in isolated areas of Magazine and Chickalah Mountain. His wife and the families of other "Mountain Feds" kept watch for movement of regular and irregular Confederates. When it was safe for him to visit, Elizabeth would place a white sheet out to dry.

Gary Varnell as bushwhacker, reenactment 2013

Most of northern and central Arkansas was no-man's land, controlled by groups of jayhawkers and bushwhackers. Generally, jayhawkers were viewed as those with Union sympathy, bushwhackers were Confederate, but often these people were just marauders, robbers, and thieves who claimed to be on the side of whomever they felt was winning. Guerrilla warfare as conducted by these outlaw bands was merciless. Murder, arson, robbery, rape, pillage and ambush were common throughout the area. Regular army troops of both sides hunted down and killed the outlaws.

Food was the most crucial problem of the war years. Farmers were urged to grow wheat and corn instead of cotton. Some soldiers even received furloughs in order to help with the crops. With both armies procuring supplies by foraging the countryside, even these crops produced in abundance before the war became scarce. Sugar, coffee, tea and other foods not produced in Arkansas were extremely expensive, sometimes not even available. For the ordinary citizen, all economic activity had ceased. The cotton fields stood fallow, the mills closed or burned. Small rural business such as sawmills, gristmills, craft-shops, and saltpeter works ceased to exist. Butter sold for $3.00 a pound in Confederate occupied areas and coffee for nearly $7 dollars per pound. Calico, which sold for a dime before the war, was already at $5.00 a yard at the end of 1863. So desperate were people for salt, soil was removed from smoke houses, mixed with water, and boiled to extract small amounts of the white gold. Corn had been readily available and cheap before the war, now it was selling for $10 a bushel. Illegal cotton trade with unscrupulous Northern merchants and even with Federal troops occurred in occupied areas.

David Chilton, Paris Reenactment 2013

As the war went on, gristmills and flour mills became special targets to be destroyed- a way of preventing the enemy from obtaining supplies. In the Ozarks and much of the Ouachita's, people often faced starvation.

Area counties suffered heavily as a result of the war. Farms lay in ruin. Houses and rail fences were burned, and uncultivated fields grew up in bushes. Blackened chimneys rose out of piles of ash, the remnants of where homes had once stood. Many people simply packed up and left, taking their families to safe areas. This was the world in which Heffington found himself during the summer of 1863. In addition to family difficulties, the "Mountain Feds," over two-hundred strong, were now in desperate straits. The "Union" men had conducted a clandestine war against the Confederacy for three years but were desperate for supplies. Heffington was close friends with many of the men and felt, correctly so, that the Union would be glad to assist these men.

Reenactment, Haguewood, 2013

"Wild Bill" and a man by the name of McBride, possibly a relative, decided to travel to Missouri to obtain assistance. On August 15, 1863, McBride stated that he separated from Heffington as they crossed the Arkansas River in Crawford County. According to local history, he was captured by confederate guerrillas and executed. Others believe he was killed and his body hidden by McBride. "Wild Bill" was never seen again.

After the turn of the century, one of the Cox family was hunting in Cox valley. Walking along a rock ledge, the man spotted a wrapped object lying between two rock layers. Retrieving and unwrapping the object, the hunter discovered a Civil War era rifle in nearly perfect condition. The rifle was smooth bore and bore some writing

Pistol found by Walter Hice family, Cox Valley

and carving but appeared to be in perfect condition. He later sold the gun to a museum in Kansas – perhaps the last residing place for "Old Silversides" and the Heffington legend.

The Battle of Haguewood Prairie

As a part of the western theater, Arkansas had few major battles which involved the movement and combat of large numbers of men. Most of northwest Arkansas had fallen to Union forces after the Battle of Prairie Groove in December of 1862.

Short Mountain from Haguewood Prairie, Geological Drawing, 1860

Federal troops occupied Fayetteville and were threatening Fort Smith by April of 1863 and then, unexpectedly, pulled troops out of the area. Advancing again in August of 1863, they eventually occupied Fort Smith and were able to maintain posts in several of the small towns up and down the Arkansas River. Small contingents of Federal troops were, at various times, stationed at Ozark, Roseville, Clarksville, Dardanelle, and near Conway.

Over seven-hundred skirmishes, engagements, and small military actions occurred throughout the state. Hundreds more were played out between small groups of marauders and bushwhackers that moved freely throughout the area. What these battles lacked in number, they made up for in ferocity, barbarity, and violence. This was especially true in much of the River Valley region- a huge lawless track of virtual no-man's land composed of people with divided loyalties. There were several small skirmishes in the region, notably in Clarksville, Roseville, on Magazine Mountain, and at Haguewood Prairie.

Typically, there are reasons why battles occur in certain places. Geography, climate, transportation, and supplies are major factors. Federal troops moved into Fort Smith on August 30, 1863 and pushed the Confederates out of Sebastian County at the battle of Backbone Ridge on September 1. Little Rock was not abandoned by the Confederacy until September 10, 1863. The only lines of supply for the men were from Kansas or by steamboat and wagon from Little Rock. Shallow waters of the Arkansas River often prevented steamboat travel west of Dardanelle for long periods during the spring and fall. When this occurred, supplies were off-loaded onto wagon and delivered to Fort Smith via the Old Military road or a road that ran along what is highway 65 on the north side of the river. The Old Military road, constructed in the 1830's, ran from Memphis, through Little Rock, and on to Norristown (Russellville) on the North side of the river. It crossed the river using ferry or steamboat to Dardanelle and then South of the River to Stinnet's Station, Paris, near Charleston, through Lavaca, and into Fort Smith. Beginning in 1858, it was a trunk line of the Butterfield Stage Company. Both the Butterfield Stage Company and the mail routes made use of stations which supplied resting places for passengers, food, and fresh horses. Known stops included Potts Tavern (Pottsville, AR.), Dardanelle, Stinnet's Station (Delaware), Creole Station (Subiaco), Moffatts Station, Charleston, and Lavaca. These stations and routes were well known by guerillas of both sides as was the route following today's highway 10 south of Magazine Mountain. Both sides raided supply wagons and small group of soldiers that were moving through the region.

The Arkansas River is the largest obstacle blocking the movement of men and supplies north and south. Generally, west of Clarksville, men and horses could find areas of the river shallow enough that they could ford the river. Taking wagons across was another matter entirely. Wagons trying to ford streams more than three feet deep often found themselves, like cars in

overflowing streams, toppled or carried distances downstream. Cavalry troops often referred to wagons as impediments since they slowed the rate of speed at which they could progress. When possible, they liked to leave them behind but, if the raid went more than

Ferry at Roseville, Logan County Historical Society

a few days, they were necessary to carry food and ammunition. The size and depth of the river then resulted in the necessity for armies to locate ferries to transfer them across the stream. The best ferries existed at Morrison Bluff, Patterson Bluff, Roseville, and Van Buren. As a result, many of the skirmishes occurred in these places.

By late 1863, the Union, at least on paper, controlled all areas north of the Arkansas River from Little Rock through Oklahoma. Rebel forces pulled south and reestablished the capital at Old Washington. The area between the two armies became burned over sections controlled by gangs of bushwhackers, jayhawkers, marauders, and just plain thieves.

General James Blunt, U.S.

Some two-hundred "Mountain Feds" had banded together in the River Valley to oppose Rebel forces. A loose confederation, these men attacked and disrupted Confederate efforts throughout the region. When large forces were sent against them, they disbanded and disappeared into the forests and rocks of Magazine and other mountains in the region. "Wild Bill" Heffington and others from this group had journeyed north in April, 1863 and joined organized Union forces. By late summer of 1863, the remaining men were running short of supplies and ammunition needed to continue the insurgency against the Confederates. Heffington, who had returned to visit his wife, was killed as he tried to deliver the message concerning needed supplies to Union forces.

As Union forces occupied Fort Smith and the surrounding area, the message got through to General Blount, commander of Union Forces in Fort Smith. Company F of the First Arkansas Infantry was composed of men that had been recruited from the Magazine Mountain region. This group consisted of several men who had been recruited from the local area and probably knew many of the "Mountain Feds" they were to assist. According to the official records, General Blunt assigned this group of men the task of delivering assistance and supplies to the Mountain Feds. They accomplished this task and, while traveling back to Fort Smith, apparently camped on Haguewood Prairie near present day Paris. The commander of the group, Captain William C. Parker, was a native of Six Mile Creek Township, had family in the area, as did many of his men. Some of his men used this opportunity to go to their homes and visit family. Other men had several family members join them at the campsite. More than likely, many of the men were planning to take these family members back with them to the safety offered by occupied Fort Smith.

Haguewood Prairie, located just east of present day Paris, was largely unsettled and consisted of a nearly treeless track of open plain traversed by Haguewood Creek and its many branches. It is also the location of several natural springs and could supply needed forage and water for man and beast. An ideal camping place, it had probably been used for years by various groups that were passing through the area.

On the morning of September 27th, 1863, the Union camp consisted of about eighty men from the First Arkansas, a few family members including several children, and possibly a handful of men from other units who, for one reason or another, were traveling with the group. Artifacts indicate that the group were camped just south of the Military Road and along Haguewood Creek. There were two military wagons and possibly some privately owned wagons, probably several tents and a number of campsites. Since it was nearly noon and the men were still encamped, no doubt they had been given the day off to complete family affairs or to rest. As they sat around the campsite, little did they realize that one of the most famous cavalry leaders of the Confederacy and his eight hundred chosen men were rapidly approaching their encampment. Before the day was over, at least seven men were killed, over twenty wounded, and many of the 1st Arkansas captured by the enemy. As we know from our various wars in Afghanistan, Iraq, and the Middle East, battles and wars are not defined by numbers of gravestones or by written words of military reports- they are determined by the people involved and how those incidents forever change their lives.

History is actually the story of people- and the real people who often make it happen are the common man- the type that has a family, goes to work each day, does his duty, and makes the best of what life pitches his way. The Battle of Haguewood Prairie offers opportunity to explore the lives of these individuals and to look beyond the rank, date, and serial number that we find in most military records. Many of the people involved in the battle were locals who became caught up in the conflict that was sweeping across the country. Some had been conscripted into the Confederacy and now had the opportunity to join forces with like-minded individuals of the 1st Arkansas. Some were just visiting loved family members or merely traveling along the pathways of the conflicting parties, and some were dedicated individuals that found glory and excitement in fighting for a cause in which they believed. Family histories, old photos and letters found in attics, diaries, and even a complete autobiography tell the story of Haguewood.

The Confederates were led by the dashing and daring soon to be General Jo Shelby. Although from Waverly, Missouri, Shelby was the epitome of the Southern Gentleman. He was born in Kentucky to a wealthy family that included Abraham Lincoln's Postmaster General Montgomery Blair. The Blair House of Washington D.C., directly across from the White House, is still used to house international VIP guests visiting the President.

General Jo Shelby

At an early age, Shelby and his stepbrothers established a hemp plantation on the Missouri River, not far from Kansas City. Even though many of his family had strong ties to the North, Shelby was a strong supporter of both slavery and state's rights. He became involved in the Bloody Kansas wars prior to the Civil War and was established as a leader of men opposed to Kansas being a free state. When the war began, he organized his own group of men and joined the war as an officer in the Confederacy.

Shelby and many of his men came from the wealthy, educated supporters of the war. He was able to purchase his own uniform, horse, and weapons. Like many of the educated young

Confederate gentlemen, he had been raised on the stories of Sir Walter Scott and war brought visions of knightly grandeur, gallantry, and heroism. Dressed in his gray uniform, saddled on his trusted bay stead, and crowned with a cavalry hat adorned with a sweeping black ostrich feather, he was a gallant and dashing figure and men flocked to join him. Shelby provided funding to outfit this group of men is a manner suitable to his style. Many of them stayed with him throughout the war and even followed him into Mexico at the conclusion of the war. This included his man-servant slave John- a Shelby follower to the bitter end. Of course, John may or may not have been as loyal as much as he was compelled to accompany Shelby into Mexico. Shelby's men fought at the battle of Wilson Creek, a battle in which his half-brother Carey was killed while fighting for the Union.

Shelby was a man who could get things done. When General Morgan needed rifle caps for his army in Kentucky, Shelby is the man who devised the ingenious method of shipping thousands of them from St. Louis embedded in containers of potted flowers. He could get more from his men and horses than was thought possible. His "Iron Brigade" could stay in saddle for days on end, living off the land, and covering fifty and more miles in a day. When pursued, he was known to line his mounted troops into long lines, take the bit from the mounts mouth, and have each trooper hold a stalk of corn extended to the horse in line behind him, allowing the horses to feed while traveling.

He led troops at both Pea Ridge and Prairie Groove. At Prairie Groove, he and a small group of his men got too far out in front of the troops and were surrounded by the enemy. He was at the point of surrendering his sword when a group of guerilla soldiers lead by none other than Frank James rode out of the darkness and rescued him. The James boys, Youngers, and Quantrill's infamous men often interacted and rode with groups of Shelby's men. Later in life when Frank was captured and brought to trail, Shelby repaid the favor by testifying in support of Frank James. Frank James beat the charges and was released- much to the surprise and anger of many whom he robbed.

One of the other remarkable stories to come from Shelby's exploits at Prairie Groove invoked the exploits of Knights of the Round Table. On December 7, 1862, Union and Confederate

Alonzo Slayback

forces at Prairie Groove faced each across an open field. Colonel Alonzo Slayback, one of Shelby's closest followers and officers, seized the moment to ride his stead into the gap between the two armies. Facing the enemy, he issued the challenge for the Union to send out a champion to face him in single combat. Quick as lightning, Captain Willhite, an Arkansas recruit, answered the challenge by riding forth on his horse. Facing each other, they waited until separated by a distance of twenty paces and then began firing. Both missed on the first shot, but Slayback inflicted a severe wound on Willhite with his second shot. Two other Federals dashed out to regain the honor of their unit. Again the sides charged- this time in groups of three as Slayback was joined by two of his own- and again a Federal soldier fell wounded from his saddle. The North then retired from the field. Slayback, suffering through a severe bout of malaria during the Great Raid, was not with Shelby at Haguewood. Slayback remained with Shelby on his journey into Mexico after the war and enough stories to fill a book have been written and told of his exploits.

Shelby was superstitious and believed that as long as he rode a bay horse, he would never fall on the battlefield. This proved to be an effective plan for him but not for his horses, he had at least five and perhaps as many as nine horses shot from under him.

The year 1863 was not a good year for the Confederacy as a whole and Arkansas in particular. Helena had been occupied by Union Forces under General Curtis in late 1862. Confederate troops were determined to reoccupy it and to also provide some relief for Confederate troops who were under siege in Vicksburg, Mississippi. General Price stormed the Port of Helena on July 4, 1863. The attack was an uncoordinated disaster and the Confederates were beaten back. While on the battlefield, General Shelby was struck by a bullet that entered his wrist and exited near his elbow. Men close to him stated that he scarcely gasped as the bullet passed through his body and he continued with his duties, although he was bleeding badly. During the subsequent retreat back to Little Rock, Shelby's arm became infected and he suffered from pain and fever during the siege of Little Rock in late August of that year.

The defeat at Helena was just one of three great disasters that occurred on July 4, 1863. Vicksburg surrendered to Grant and the huge loss at Gettysburg by the South on the same day spelled the eventual demise of the Confederacy.

Shelby and the Confederates were forced to surrender Little Rock in August of 1863 with scarcely a shot being fired. Arkansas's army and government were moved to Washington, Arkansas.

Shelby was a man of action. No doubt, he was dissatisfied with the direction the war was taking and discouraged by the actions taken by his superiors. He felt that a brave, daring strike into the heart of Missouri would revitalize the spirit of his troops, allow him to obtain needed supplies, and provide him a base from which to obtain new recruits. Few of his superiors agreed with his beliefs but his persistence resulted in him obtaining support from Missouri Governor Reynolds and eventually General Price. Instead of allowing him his entire command, the agreement was to provide him only eight-hundred men, some of whom he would have to collect as he moved northward.

On September 22, 1863, Shelby and troops filed through Arkadelphia past Missouri Confederate Governor Thomas Reynolds, General Sterling Price, and other officials, beginning a journey that would take them more than seven hundred miles into enemy territory.

More than thirty-thousand Union forces were stationed in Arkansas along and north of the Arkansas River. Along with Shelby's eight hundred man cavalry, he had twelve ammunition wagons and two pieces of artillery which restricted where and how he could travel. Horses and men could traverse streams and rivers by swimming, the wagons and artillery required ferries or the construction of rafts. Federal troops were known to be stationed at Dardanelle, Clarksville, and Fort Smith. Shelby directed his troops toward Roseville.

Once considered as the site of the state capital, Roseville was a thriving Franklin county farm community located on the Arkansas River and had an excellent river crossing, port, and shallow ferry. Even more importantly, few or no Union soldiers were expected to block their passage across the river.

Other than a skirmish with a large group of bushwhackers near Caddo Gap, Shelby meet little resistance on the one-hundred and fifty mile leg of journey to cross the Arkansas. It is believed that his journey included back roads that brought him from Arkadelphia, through Caddo Gap, northward to Danville, across Harkey's Valley, and then to Shoal Creek, located on the Old Military Road. Tradition and family histories state that he camped on the south side of PeeDee Creek at what is now known as the Artesian Well on September 26, 1863. As he and his men

44

bedded down for the night, little did he know that the First Arkansas Infantry was doing the same only twelve miles up the road.

Captain William C. Parker of the 1st Arkansas Infantry probably felt much at home that same night as he and his group bedded down at Haguewood Creek. With some eighty men, he had successfully delivered two wagon loads of military equipment to the "Mountain Feds." From the amount of solid bricks of lead found on site, the military goods no doubt consisted of sufficient amounts of powder and shot. He had allowed several of his men to visit families located in the area. Other soldiers from Arkansas units must have accompanied him on the trip or have been on furlough in the area since Captain James LaFerry and Captain James Garner have reported involvement in the battle. In addition, several men had family members with them. These families included the Hawkins, Plumley, and others whose intentions were probably to accompany the First Infantry back to the safety of Fort Smith.

Parker owned land around Six Mile Creek and he had several family members who lived nearby.

Joyce Friddle at her ancestor, James Garners Hideout on Red Bench

According to family history, his father William Samuel Parker, had been a veteran of the Mexican War so he came from a family with a military background. When the war began, he was a part of the 58th militia that consisted of men from south Franklin County. He is listed as First Lieutenant for that group during its inspection and drill held in February and March of 1862. It is not known if he was active in this Confederate unit but his wife, Eliza J. (Brown) Parker later filed for and received benefits as a Confederate soldier. Perhaps he was an unwilling participant or became disenchanted with the war but, for whatever reason, he enlisted for a three year period in

Company E, 1st Arkansas Cavalry in July of 1862. Even at twenty-three years of age, he must have shown leadership qualities because he was quickly moved to the position of Sargent. He was mustered into service in Springfield, Missouri. He was detailed to a recruiting service for the 1st Arkansas Infantry in March, 1863 and then, in April, discharged to accept an appointment in the 1st Arkansas Infantry. Since these men were primarily people from Franklin and Johnson County, it could be assumed he recruited and then joined the group of men from his home area- part of the "Mountain Feds."

He is cited for heroism at the Battle of Fayetteville in April, 1863 where he received a slight wound to his head.

Fort Smith fell to the Union on the last day of August of 1863. The 1st were part of the group assigned to guard and maintain Fort Smith and the surrounding region. The Mountain Feds had been assisting the Union cause for over two years. Working out of mountain hideouts on Magazine, Short, and Rich Mountain, they had attacked and harassed the Confederate lines of supplies and communication all along the river. By late summer, they were in dire straits and low on goods and ammunition. Captain Parker and his men had provided that help, now they were enjoying the opportunity of visiting their homeland.

Mahalia Laferry Plunkett, neice of Capt. James Laferry, 1868 photo

With Parker was Captain James Laffery. The thirty-nine year old Laffery, a veteran of the Mexican War, had just been appointed captain in the 4th Arkansas Cavalry. Laffery owned property in several locations in what was to become Logan County. He owned part of a section

46

of property near Baxter cemetery just north of Paris and three-hundred and eighteen acres of land near Ellsworth, a rather substantial community located on the Military road just west of present day Midway.

With his prior experience, Laffery was a welcome addition to the group. He had experienced war first-hand in Missouri where he was involved in several skirmishes. He had been captured and was released on parole in February of 1863. Later, he was involved in battles at Fayetteville, Fort Smith, Dardanelle, and Honey Springs, Oklahoma. During his lifetime, he is said to have participated in more than forty battles.

He and his wife, the former Martha Smith, had a number of children including George, Mary Ann, Margaret, Catherine, Nancy, Julia, Curley, Josiah, James, Reuben and Amanda (twins), Mattie and Virginia and, more than likely he came along with the 1st Infantry in order to visit with his family.

Captain James Garner owned forty acres of land just south of Paris on Red Bench Road near the small town of Revelee. In 1859, he paid thirty dollars for the

Captain James Garner

Emily Barnes Garner

property and began farming the land. A large mill was located on Cutter Creek near his home. Although he owned the mill at some point, during the war it was ran by the Lee Family. Mills were favorite targets for both armies during the war. Powered by water, they provided the energy to convert corn into meal, an essential part of the diet for people of the south. In addition, sawmills, planers, and shake mills were often

powered by the same source. Water mills were often the first things destroyed when the enemy

moved into an area so Garner and his family would have been prime targets of the Confederates.

He, like Laferry, was a family man and a

veteran of the Mexican War. When provided

the opportunity, he would return home to visit

with his family. Because the region was so

divided in loyalty, he usually stayed in a hide-

out cave located above his property.

Accessing his hideout, one would be protected

Mill Pond, Cutter Creek from the south by a large bluff line. On the north,

one could see the approach of any enemy and escape long before they arrived. From the heights,

he could see his home on the bench below and his wife Emily would let him know when it was

safe to visit. He could then slip through the forest and join them for short visits. Uncomfortable

as it must have been, Garner spent many nights hid out in this hideaway. It is very likely that he

was taking the opportunity to visit the family on the night of September 26, 1863.

As was his custom, Shelby and his men would have been up and on their way at daybreak. With

twelve wagons, two cannon, and eight hundred mounted men, they would have been an

impressive sight as they traveled up the Old Military road. If they rode two abreast and spread

out even ten or so feet apart, the column would have stretched for more than a half-mile. Most

of the men were dressed in cast-off and captured Union blue uniforms or whatever clothing they

were able to obtain from foraging. Shelby once remarked that he and his men were never issued

one uniform by the Confederate army during the entire war so he felt totally justified in using whatever clothing he could obtain. In fact, Edwards states that during this campaign Shelby's men rode with sumac leaves in their hats so they could distinguish themselves from the enemy. The officers dressed with daring and flare, wearing cavalry hats with sweeping ostrich feathers and uniforms with bright sashes of color. Each company would have individual bright colored flags and these, as well as the Confederate flag, would have been flying in the breeze as Shelby and his men moved rapidly westward. The group would have posed a colorful and romantic sight to the isolated communities and farms through which they passed.

Edwards reports that they were fired upon several times from ambush as they traveled, no doubt by the refurbished Mountain Feds that were to be found throughout the area. Shelby always sent scouts out in advance of his main force. It was the job of these scouts to detect the enemy and root out these small pockets of opposition. The leader of his scouts, Captain "Tuck" Thorpe, was known for his daring and bravery. His instructions were to never retreat- to do so would lead the enemy straight back into the

Student Re-enactors at Haguewood Prairie

unprepared cavalry. Thorpe was instructed to take the fight to the enemy, stand his ground and fire, and Shelby and his men would come as quickly as possible to the battle.

The Confederates made good time, traveling some eight or nine miles west by noon. It was probably a shock to both sides when Thorpe and his men trotted over a slight rise along Hagwood Creek and saw an encampment of several tents, wagons, and more than eighty men. Intermingled with the men of the 1st Infantry were several local citizens, including women and

49

children. Immediately, both sides began firing and the men of the 1st dropped back into the protection of the tree line along the creek. Private Isaac Plumley was hit in the leg as he struggled to get his wife and three daughters to safety behind a large tree.

Johnathan Edwards, Shelby's adjunct and biographer.

Shelby heard the firing in his advance and quickly moved him men forward into battle position. Seeing the enemy ensconced within the tree line, he ordered his men to dismount and fire from the ground. Evidence from materials retrieved from the battle scene validates many of the historical documents and stories about Southern Cavalry. Most of the men would have found it difficult to fire the common 60 caliber rifles generally used by the South and would have instead used pistols, often carrying two of more of the revolvers with them. Most of these revolvers were of small 36 caliber but were very accurate for close-up fighting and had interchangeable cylinders containing six shot. Many of the men also brought shotguns with them from home. These shotguns were filled with fragments of iron, lead shot, or whatever was available. The disadvantage, as Shelby's troops soon discovered, was that the range of their weapons was very limited. Many of the 1st Infantry had obtained castoff Springfield rifles left on the field at Prairie Groove. These rifles were very accurate, shot 58 caliber minie or round shot, and had a range of up to 500 yards. As the battle raged into its second hour, Shelby succinctly describes his actions:

> *"I immediately ordered two regiments to dismount, who skirmished with them until [G. P.] Gordon and [David] Shanks got on either flank, when a simultaneous charge scattered them like chaff, and our rough riders rode them down like stubble to the lava tide."*

It is not known whether Shelby fired either of his two cannons on the battle field. Two 6 pound cannon balls and the tie chain for a caisson were found on the battlefield. The terrain around Hagwood Creek was and is very rugged and, since all three were found in the same location, it is assumed that they were lost during the confusion of the battle. Either way, the Shelby's charge quickly overwhelmed the Union opposition but left at least five rebel soldiers dead on the field as well as wounding several others.

The Fort Smith newspaper, *The New Era,* reports that Pvt. Benjamin Wilkins *"....fell pierced with several bullets, bravely discharging his six-shooter and killing one of his assailants."* Wilkins was a local man, brother in law to Captain James Garner, and owned a farm just a short distance from where the battle occurred. Wilkins death left a wife and several small children in a destitute situation, one that his young wife had difficulty in managing. The children were raised to adulthood in the home of Wilkins brother-in-law, the aforementioned James and Emily

John H. Wilkins Family — Back: John H. and Mary Etta Wilkins. Front: Archie Blaine, Pearl, Maude, Elmo.

Garner. In the <u>Biographical and Historical Memoirs of Northwest Arkansas</u>, John Wilkins, Benjamin's son, is described as a successful merchant and property owner in Paris, Arkansas.

The other Union casualty was Pvt. William Hawkins. Hawkins retreated into one of the wagons, fighting to protect his sister who had joined the Union men in order to escape to Fort Smith. She watched from the wagon as Hawkins was gunned down by the enemy. Shelby and his men rounded up twenty-eight men from the 1st Infantry as well as nearly a dozen civilians. Captain Parker was able to escape but most of his officers, including James Laferry, were captured.

Rachael (Plumlee) McChristian at Haguewood dedication

Pvt. Isaac Plumlee was wounded during the battle. Isaac, a farmer from Carrol County, had ten children prior to the war. His oldest son William was also a member of the 1st Infantry and he, as well as several of Isaac's other ten children, were with him, possibly accompanying the group into Fort Smith. As described by Edwards, Plumlee had received a substantial wound and was lying beneath a large tree on the battlefield. His daughters were gathered about him, weeping and calling plaintively to their father, "Daddy, oh dad, you look so pale. Oh dad, are you going to be all right." Shelby overheard what was going on and, moved by the plight of the family, he pulled gold coin from his own pocket. "I can't make your dad all right but this will help to get you through," he stated, laying the money in the families hands. Other of the soldiers followed suit, presenting paper and gold to the family. Plumlee was transferred to a hospital in Fort Smith where he was eventually released from service with a 70% disability and a large sum of money given to him by his enemy. It was stated that he made more in that one afternoon than he would have made in the entire war as a soldier. The injury certainly did not affect his virility; he remarried after the war and had seven more children, the last born when he was sixty-three years of age.

Daniel R. Lee, his wife Susan (Redden) Lee, and children lived near the battlefield on the property now owned by Gordon (Butch) Baker. Daniel's thirteen year old son Thomas was wandering down the road behind his property when he met up with a group of Confederates in an ammunition wagon. Two deep, clear springs lie on the back of the present day Davis property. These springs, used for years as a water source, are very clear and never go dry. Some of Shelby's troops were familiar with the region and were probably using the spring to obtain fresh drinking water during the warm September day. Several ingots of lead and other materials were found near the site. The road traveled by young Lee passed very close to the springs. The Confederates compelled young Thomas to join them. As they started across the creek, one of the

Daniel R. & Susan Redding Lee

soldiers took compassion on the young boy and helped him to escape by cutting the traces of the lead mule and sending it galloping and baying as it ran to the west. Thomas circled back to his home and, fearing the rebels were in pursuit, Daniel and Thomas started up the "grapevine" trail over Pine Ridge and Rich Mountain. They were ambushed as they followed the trail

53

and Daniel received a bullet wound in the chest. They escaped pursuit by hiding in the underbrush but Daniel was in much pain from the wound. Young Tom inserted a knife blade into the wound and was able to relieve the pain enough for Daniel to escape to a safe hiding place where he received proper care. The Lee's were well known for their Union sympathies and several of their family fought for the North. Scattered from Paint Rock community to Millard on Shoal Creek, Thomas and Daniel had many places from which to choose when it came to hiding out.

Daniel Lee lived for more than thirty years after the war and is buried in Moore cemetery in Greasy Valley. Some of his family is buried in a cemetery plot on the north side of Butch Bakers property. Thomas married and built a home at Millard and is ancestor to many of the Lee family living near Corley.

Shelby captured twenty-eight men and ten civilians. All of these were paroled except for John Little, a Confederate deserter who had joined the 1st Infantry and the four officers. Captain Parker had escaped; he and most of the men straggled into Fort Smith over the next couple of days. Shelby eventually released the officer when he reached Missouri but told the officers he was executing Little. He may have just told the officers this to scare them into honoring their parole since the official records state Little as eventually returned to service, rising to the rank of sergeant before being mustered out at the end of the war.

Nothing is known concerning the burial of the rebels killed in the battle. It is possible that Shelby had the bodies returned to Arkadelphia but, given the distance to Rebel lines, they are probably buried somewhere in the area.

Cavalry at Haguewood

Shelby proceeded west up the military road, perhaps to Point Prairie on Six mile creek. He arrived at Roseville before dark and states that he easily crossed the river in a shallow, sandy area. Because of depth, it would be reasonable to conclude that he used the ferry to transport the fifteen wagons that he now had. The two cannon probably had barrels stuffed with cloth and pulled across by horses, a common method of transporting cannon in the shallow rivers and streams. Upon reaching the north bank, he sent scouts toward Clarksville and Fort Smith to check on the approach of enemy and to cut telegraph lines. He and his men divided the commissary and supplies in the captured wagons and burned them. After a brief rest, probably in the area of Denning, they proceeded to Ozark and passed through the town at about daylight on the 28th. They rode to the Mulberry River (Turner Bend) where they rested their horses for a day before proceeding through the Ozarks. Shelby, dressed in best uniform and with feathered hat on his head, trotted down Main Street in Huntsville with his men strung out in file behind him. Union supporters carefully counted his men so they could report the number to Union authorities. The numbers were vastly overstated- Shelby had several of his men circle the town, join the stragglers at the end of the column, and were counted two or three times. By the time he reached the Missouri border, he was reported to have more than two thousand troops.

During his forty-one day raid into Missouri, Shelby captured 40 Federal unit banners, 600 guns, 600 revolvers, new Federal uniforms and horses, killed or wounded 600 Federal troops, paroled 500 Federal troops, destroyed two forts, miles of railroad track and telegraph lines, and destroyed property valued at more than two million dollars. Many biographers also feel that Shelby was able to tie up the more than 100,000 troops commanded by General Schofield of Missouri and over 30,000 troops in Arkansas under General Steele and prevented them from assisting in reinforcing General Rosecrans who was badly in need of reinforcements in his Tennessee Campaign.

The battle was over, the Union scattered, the Confederates successful in what became known as "The Great Raid." A winter of hardship and another year of war awaited the people of the desolate land.

Frozen Tower Moore

A Desolate Land

By late 1863, Confederate forces west of the Mississippi were in disarray. Most of the troops in Arkansas had been pulled south of the Ouachita Mountains with headquarters at Old Washington. Northern troops occupied Arkansas north of the Arkansas River but, outside of major town, their hold was tenuous at best. Guerilla, jayhawkers, and bushwhackers roamed the countryside, pillaging and burning property of both sides. Often, these men were nothing more than common thieves and crooks, taking advantage of the lawless conditions that existed throughout Missouri and Arkansas. People traveling through Southern Missouri and Northern Arkansas described a desolate land. Abandoned farms, burned homes with charred chimneys dotted the country side. Union commanders encouraged farmers to move into protected communities- and regarded those that refused as Southern sympathizers.

Property and control constantly changed hands and people in the area had a difficult time determining loyalty. If you "came out" for one side or the other, when control changed hands, your life was endangered. It also left one open to attacks from neighbors with opposing points of view. River Valley people of Northern sympathy moved their families into Fort Smith, those favoring the South often moved to Arkadelphia, Camden, or even into Texas. Those left, both those favoring Union and Confederacy, found life difficult and were often preyed on by troops of both sides. An article from the "*New Era*" newspaper of Fort Smith offers a vivid description:

November 14, 1863

PROSPECT OF THE FARMERS- BUSH-WHACKING

The town is full of refugees from the country, of whom a large number is supported by the Government. This is deplorable, not so much on the expense of feeding them, as from the injury to the community at large is receiving by the almost total suspension of farming operations. The cause of all this is bush-whacking. No family, known to entertain Union feelings, is safe out of the reach of U S Troops. The recent advance of the rebels encouraged this abominable, fiendish set of men to extend their operations nearer to town than ever. Since the hasty flight of the rebels these fiends have also become less bold in the immediate vicinity of this place. But there is still so great a feeling of insecurity among the country people, that they are very little disposed to work in good earnest and prepare another years' crop. Many families also had their houses burnt, after having been robbed of everything, and have come to town in most pitiable circumstances. The inauguration of the guerrilla warfare, is one of the deepest stains of infamy to be charged to this hellish Confederacy; for, while it decides nothing eventually, it inflicts infinitely more suffering, and especially on the helpless, than an open and regular system of warfare. Good judges estimated the amount of grain raised this year in Arkansas sufficient to bread the people for two years. Owing to the presence of large forces in the State, and the great waste and destruction caused by the rebels, we may consider ourselves fortunate if the supply holds out till next harvest. But, if we don't sow now, we can have no harvest next year, when there will be

ten times more applications for rations than now, and the suffering among

the people must necessarily be great. The only remedy is, to clean out the

bush-whackers, and give them no mercy wherever and whenever found; and then,

and not until then, may we look for a revival of prosperity.

The winter of 1863 was extremely cold and harsh. Both armies had foraged through the countryside and removed all the grain, livestock, and food they could find. So many mills had been destroyed that people were using coffee grinders or mashing the corn in a manner of Indians to make cornmeal. Salt was of extreme scarcity. One woman in Harkey Valley described how the bushwhackers that foraged her property could not find any food so they scrapped soil from beneath the smoke house to obtain the salt left from curing meat.

Prior to the war, Arkansas produced abundant crops to feed the population plus large amounts to be sold at market. During the war, the population could not feed themselves and relied on food brought in from the North to feed the population. Prices for essentials such as coffee, flour, salt, and spices were outrageous. Coffee, if available at all, sold for up to $18 per pound, butter for

$5 per pound, and calico was $5 per yard. Supplies of essentials were cheaper for those on the Union side, but were often difficult to obtain because the Confederates disrupted all of the supply lines. Bushwhackers and foraging soldiers confiscated anything they wanted

from the farms they ran across and did not limit themselves to food items. They often stole anything of value; even items of clothing, bedding, knick-knacks, and furniture. In some instances, they rounded up and wantonly killed livestock to deprive the opposition from having access to it in the future. No family or their property was secure. Even if you were on the same side as the foragers, they would often take goods and leave a script that could be turned in later for payment. Women had a difficult time maintaining the land, carrying for the children, plowing, harvesting, and the myriad other chores they had to accomplish while their husband was away.

Three deserters found refuge in a cliff above Indian Creek near Turner Bend. The area had been a hot-bed of discontent with families divided almost equally on the issue of state's rights. During the war, armies of both sides traveled through the valley on the way to battles at Wilson Creek, Missouri, Prairie Groove, and at Pea Ridge, Arkansas. In September of 1863, General Jo Shelby and his troops spent a couple of days recuperating along the Mulberry River at the conclusion of the Battle of Haguewood Prairie and before travelling northward on their Great Raid. Bushwhackers from both sides frequented the area. By 1864 and early 1865, the area was, at least on paper, in the hands of the Union. The three deserters, at least one of which was local, were just trying to survive and last out the war. Hiding under the cliff in a secluded area, they raided farms along the Mulberry for food and supplies. Many such cliffs had been used during the Civil War for shelter and safety. Located half-way up the mountainside, the shelter offered virtual protection on three sides and a wide –open viewing area that provided opportunity to spot any enemy long before they arrived. The grotto-type overhang provided protection and shelter from inclement weather and a location that was warm in the winter and cool in the summer. Local home guards were alerted to their presence and were able to slip down the steep incline from above and surprise the three men. Two were killed on the spot but the third sprang down the steep incline and tumbled toward the creek below. During flight, one of the bullets clipped his boot, removing the heel. Not slowing, the desperate deserter fled down the creek and escaped. In 1870, he returned to carve a memorial to his last friends. The sad reminder of the untold deaths of the Civil War remains in the depths of the isolated National Forest site. The inscription reads; Under this bluff last lay MC, VS, and JM in 1865. A few months later, the war ended and the only reminder of this tragic loss is this memorial carved by the survivor who returned to again record his initials and the date, April 28, 1870.

One of the more prominent families in the Havana area was the Coopers. John Cooper, one of the original settlers of the state had traveled down the Mississippi River during the New Madrid Earthquake of 1812. He experienced and survived the effects of the earthquake while traveling

on the river. Arriving at Arkansas Post, he ascended the Arkansas River to Morrison's Bluff and then transported his family, slaves, and household goods across the mountain range and settled on Cedar Creek. During the war, his pregnant daughter Martha Ann (Cooper) Smith was home alone when

Old Military Road at Short Mountain

several Union bushwhackers rode up to her home. Fearing the results of their visit, she climbed into bed and began to wail away, acting as if she was in immediate labor. Expecting the imminent arrival of a child, the soldiers quickly found reason to travel on down the road to another home, leaving the

61

Joseph Horn of Midway

household untouched. Several months later, she delivered the baby, either Theodocia or William H. Smith.

South of the mountain and along Shoal Creek, many of the men joined the 4th Arkansas Cavalry (U.S.). Many of these men were native of Hamilton or Bledsoe County, Tennessee whom had moved to Arkansas and settled near each other. Over the years, the group appears to have developed closer ties through intermarriage and to also have fostered very close political views. Many of the men were conscripted into Confederate forces early in the war but switched sides at the first opportunity. A roster of names would appear very familiar to today's residents. These include the Hixson, Ezell, Trusty, Horn, Stewart, Sims, Lasater, Moore's, Rober(t)son's, and others. The group was organized in Little Rock during the fall of 1863 and Captain James Laferry was appointed the captain of the group. Laferry, the same individual who had participated at Haguewood, was a prominent landowner in the Ellsworth Community.

There were some obvious perks of being involved in the Cavalry – the foremost being mobility and having a beast to carry the accoutrements of war rather than oneself. The prerequisite to joining in Arkansas appears to be ownership of a horse. Horses were rather expensive with the average price appearing to be in the neighborhood of $150 up for a good stead- a substantial amount of money in 1860. Obviously, some men of the 4th were mounted on less stellar beasts-the value of Joseph Horn's horse is listed as $60. This might account for his spending a good part of the war cooking and caring for the ill at the company headquarters in Little Rock. Typical pay for a private was $12 dollars per month. Recruits were also provided forty cents a day for their horse. During months having thirty-one days, the horse made more than the private. War was especially difficult on the women and children left at home. Most able men were away at war, leaving the farming to the elderly, the infirm, the children, and especially, the women.

Virtually dependent on the crops and animals they could grow, they had to break, plow, plant, and harvest a crop that would feed their families while the husband was away. Even if the husband had military pay, it was extremely difficult to get it delivered to their families. In the event, the husband was in the Confederacy, the money sent home was script that was virtually useless. With both armies foraging through the countryside, not only did food become scarce but, with both sides confiscating animals, there was no way to prepare the land for farming. Joseph Horn and his brother Henry were native of Bledsoe County Tennessee. They moved to Arkansas and settled as farmers on the ridge and valley just south of what is today Midway. Joseph, the older of the two at 32 years of age, had married Ruthie Box Sims in 1855 before moving to Arkansas. He was originally a part of Captain Turners 16th Infantry, CSA. Like many others of the region, he was probably a conscript and dragged into a conflict he wished to avoid. While it is not known for sure when and how several of these men changed from CSA to USA troops, it is known that General Fagan stated that entire groups of his men deserted at the Battle of Backbone Mountain in Greenwood in September of 1863 and immediately joined ranks with Union forces, in fact fighting against him at Dardanelle only weeks later. A quick glance at enlistments of the 4th Arkansas Cavalry shows that many of the men enlisted in Fort Smith on September 15, 1863, immediately after this battle. The Horn's, their neighbors the Lasaster's, and other Shoal Creek residents were among the group entering service on those dates.

According to family history, Ruthie Sims Horn had a difficult time during the war. The home site sits on a rocky ridge and would have been difficult to farm in the best of times; virtually impossible without animals and equipment. She

Sandstone Crypts, Hickory Groove Cemetery

63

had the added difficulty of caring for several young children while she attempted to farm. To keep the young children safe in the home while she carried out the numerous required chores, she would lift the heavy cast iron bed, insert the children's gowns under the legs of the bed, and leave them with the weight of the bed holding them safely until she could return. She lost one of her children during this time. Ruthie had to dig out the shallow grave and bury her son- the first of many to be buried in Horn Cemetery.

According to family histories, many of the older cemetaries in the county have stone covered crypts covering graves from the Civil War period. These crypts are found at Hickory Groove, at Millard, and several other sites. Soils on the ridges and valleys of Magazine are thin, consisting of shale covering layers of hardened sandstone. During the war, women and children found it extremely difficult to dig deep graves. Fearing that wolves or other wild animals would dig up the graves, they used thin layers of native flagstone to surround the grave and then placed a lid over those stone, creating a closed crypt.

"Decoration Days," annual events in rural areas of the South, are held on Sundays in late spring or early summer. This tradition is especially true of mountain regions and began as families

Elias Turner, CSA

remembered lost loved ones who died during the Civil War. It has been extended to remembrances of all family and ancestors and involves placing flowers and other tokens of remembrance on the graves. Sometimes, people travel hundreds of miles to return to these services and it serves as a family homecoming. There is often a religious service and some groups conclude the day with a family potluck dinner. Some believe the traditions of this day date back to the ancient Celts, ancestors too many of the "mountain people."

Elias Turner, though a native of Franklin County, is associated with many of the men from the River Valley because he was a member of the 7th Arkansas Militia, of what we would today call the National Guard of Franklin County. Since Logan County was formed from pieces of several counties and was not in existence in 1860, many men in the shadow of Magazine Mountain were originally a part of the same group.

He was born in Perry County, Tennessee on January 24, 1830 and moved to Franklin County, Arkansas in 1853. He enlisted in Company K of the 4th Arkansas Cavalry Regiment (CSA) as Private after leaving the militia and was later promoted to 3rd Lieutenant. The more interesting stories involving him occurred after the war. He was county Judge in Franklin County from 1874 to 1878. His last official act as County Judge was the granting of a license for sale of "Intoxicating Liquor" in Ozark, one of the few "wet" counties to allowing sale of wine, beer, and hard liquor. He later served in the state legislature as State Representative.

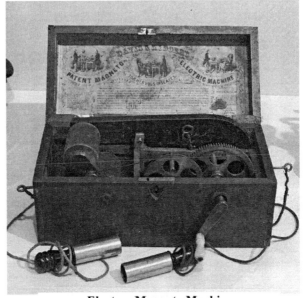

Electro- Magneto Machine

Elias died after a night at a fair. Travelling fairs at that time offered a variety of attractions, many involving the use of new "sciences" that were a part of the World Fairs. Later, this included such things as X-ray machines (which caused high rates of cancer for the people who subjected themselves to numerous photo's), prototypes of automobiles, and even telephones. In the 1880's, electricity was the vogue and the fair had a booth with an electric magneto. These consisted of two medal cylinders connected to opposite poles of an electric generator. The operator challenged individuals to hold onto the cylinders while he cranked the generator and created a charge. Turner accepted the challenge and proved to be quite capable of absorbing charge. He bested all challengers and wore the operator out. On the way home he began feeling faint. Turning to his oldest son John, he muttered, " I think I've killed myself." Evidently he felt a pressure or irregularity in his heart. At any rate, Elias survived all of the Civil War and the hardships it brought only to be found deceased in his bed the next morning.   Elias is buried in the John Huggins Cemetery, Franklin County, Arkansas.

Hansel Benjamin Trusty was another Tennessee native that was caught up in the troubles that afflicted the River Valley during the war. He was born in 1832 to Hansel G. Trusty and Catherine Biter. At age 13, he was hired out to a work with a traveling crew made of slaves and indentured whites. Working alongside the crew, he was repulsed by the action of the overseer toward the slaves and, at the first opportunity, ran off. Hansel ended up fleeing to Arkansas where he remained for two years before returning to his Tennessee. He found both of his parents had died from cholera. Deciding to return to Arkansas, he talked his brother Henry into moving to Crowley's Ridge along with him. He married Martha Ditton in 1854 and began his first family.   Prior to the war, he moved near Ellsworth and began farming. He was a prosperous in his work, joined the local Masonic lodge, and probably was a member of the local militia since he was a member of the Confederate forces at the Battle of Pea Ridge and at Helena. Hansel's experience with the slave gang had shaped his opinion concerning slavery and he was an adamant abolitionist. No doubt, he joined the Confederacy out of state pride or because he was compelled to. At some point he deserted the Confederacy, possibly after the Battle of Backbone Ridge. On Nov. 14, 1863 he joined the 4th Arkansas Cavalry at Dardanelle.

In the 4th Cavalry, he would have met up with several old acquaintances including Pleasant Stewart, Joseph Horn, several of the Hixson family, and his old neighbor, Lovett Hibbs. He served the remainder of the war with the 4th and was involved in several of the battles and skirmishes that occurred throughout the River Valley. At the completion of the war, Trusty, like several of his neighbors, was eligible to draw benefits from both armies.

Several local men were not as lucky. Matt Hixson of Shoal Creek enlisted as a corporal in the Confederate Army in 1861. He took part in the battle of Corinth, Elk Horn, and at Port Hudson and was twice wounded, once in the chest but the bullet was nearly spent and did little damage. At Port Hudson, he was captured and taken to Johnson Island, Ohio.

U. S. MILITARY PRISON JOHNSON'S ISLAND, LAKE ERIE, OHIO.

He remained at Johnson Island for about ten months. During that period of time, he suffered a bout of small-pox. Later, he was told he was being transported to Point Lookout, Md. to be exchanged. Instead, he was not exchanged and ended up in a prison in South Carolina where he was once fired upon by both sides. Conditions within prisons of both forces were horrible and rift with disease and starvation. During one bleak period, Mr. Hixson and his comrades captured and smothered a small dog brought on base by a visitor. They cleaned the carcass and boiled it in a tea kettle to supplement their daily allowance of one piece of cornbread, pickles, and whatever vegetables were available. Many of the caretakers at the prison were former slaves who had enlisted in the military. Once, while diving for oysters in the shallow water around the prison, a guard recognized his former master buried in the mud seeking for food, Hello, Massa, w'at yo doing down dar?" to which his master replied, explaining his situation. The guard than exclaimed, pointing at himself, " I used to be the bottom rail, now bottom rail on the top."

Several of the Varnell family was captured while fighting in Georgia. Three of them ended up in the notorious prison camp at Andersonville. More than 45,000 Union troops were incarcerated there and 13,000 of them died. Conditions at the prison were some of the worst known in history. Captain Hartmann Heinrich "Henry" Wirz, commander of the prison, was hanged after the war for the atrocities he committed.

The Varnell boys survived the war and, upon release, had the misfortune to be assigned to the SS Sultana for delivery home.

The *Sultana* was a Mississippi River side-wheel steamboat that was being used to transport released prisoners back home. The boat was tremendously overloaded and its four steam boilers exploded and the ship sank shortly after it left port in Memphis on April 27th, 1865. It became the greatest maritime disasters in United States history when an estimated 1,800 of its 2,427 died in the explosion. The Varnell boys were sleeping on the deck and were all able to escape and swim to safety. Josiah received severe burns from the steam and was afflicted from the scarring for the rest of his life.

Magazine Mountain is the center of a number of east-west folded mountains. The folds form numerous ridges and valleys throughout the region. Early settlers, moving into the area searched for water from springs, creeks, and small rivers. Any piece of land having water and that looked fertile enough to grow a crop, and some that did not, were purchased as homesteads and the benches, ridges, and valleys were named for the principal inhabitant. In 1837, Henry W. Ferguson, his wife Elizabeth, and numerous of his children were again on the move. Henry was born in South Carolina in 1793, the son of a Revolutionary War soldier. He later lived in Kentucky, Tennessee, and Missouri before moving with his family to an area near War Eagle mill. In 1847, he and his extended family were again on the move with Texas as the final destination. Passing through what was then Scott County, Arkansas, one of the oxen died and he had no replacement. A squatter had built a small cabin and had begun a farm in the area where Ferguson lost his oxen. Ferguson, either attracted to the land by its beauty or by necessity to stop for the winter, purchased the land. Before his death during the spring of 1848, he broke the land and planted a crop of corn. His wife and extended family stayed on the site that became known as Ferguson Valley, many remaining there until this day.

Mrs. Ferguson was a "granny" woman, a person good with herbs, healing poultices, and delivering children. She continued as midwife and doctor for the community until her death in 1870. She and Henry had eleven known children and most of them were either with their parents when they settled or followed their parents to the Valley.

Their family history during the Civil War mimic's that of many of the area's inhabitants. The Ferguson family was known to be of Union sympathy. Nevertheless, Lewis was conscripted into the Confederacy and was shot while trying to escape and was buried near where he was killed, in the Springhill Cemetery near Chismville. James, another of the brothers, was also killed by Rebel forces.

William "Billy" Ferguson

One of the daughters, Susan, had passed away in 1862. She had married William Damron and had three children. After her death, William Damron had remarried but two of the boys often stayed with their Uncle William. Damron, threatened by bushwhackers, tried to escape down the Arkansas River on boat. The boat, Damron, and eleven year old Julie were never heard of again.

Another of the boys, John "Blackjack" Ferguson, joined Union forces and served in the United States 1st Regiment, Arkansas Cavalry, Company C. His date of enlistment is July 14, 1862 and he lists his place of birth as Fentress County, Tennessee. During the war John moved his family to Fort Smith to avoid attacks by bushwhackers. After the war, they returned to their home in the Blackjack community, where they lived for the remainder of John's life

Oldest son William, after repeated attacks by the bushwhackers, decided it was time to flee the community. While trying to escape, he was shot and severely wounded in the leg. He was taken to the post in Fort Smith to recover. It was probably at this time that his younger sister Nancy Jane and mother appealed to the Union for assistance. In her deposition, she testified about the attacks by bushwhackers and about the constant foraging by the Union Army which created desperate circumstances for the families in the Valley.

" I went to Fort Smith myself to get the train to come out to move these families to the post. We had all been threatened by the rebels and were afraid to remain at home any longer. I went to the Provost Marshall and got him to send along with the forage train some extra wagons to move the families to Fort Smith."

A few months later, William traveled to Southern Illinois to stay with his brother Thomas, a physician in Marion, Illinois. According to family tradition, William traveled ahead with two of his children, John Wesley and Susan Elizabeth. His wife, Abigail, followed later with the remaining children. While enroute to Illinois by means of a river boat, the family was stricken with measles. Abigail, James, and a younger child died and were buried on the banks of the White River. Sarah was eventually returned to William. This information was passed down through family and later much of it was

Dr. Thomas D. Ferguson of Illinois

confirmed by William's Southern Claims Commission deposition.

In the summer of 1864, William returned to Arkansas and worked at the garrison in Fort Smith. He left his children temporarily with his brother in Illinois until he could prepare a home for them to return to. All of his buildings had been burned by bushwhackers, after removal of William's family, with the exception of a corn crib. When the family returned to Scott County,

71

Elizabeth Wisdom Ferguson

they lived in the corn crib until a house could be built.

William later married Elizabeth Wisdom Ferguson and had four more children; Martha, Mary Ann, William H., and Frances.

William lived the remainder of his life as a farmer in Ferguson Valley, and worked hard with other men in the community to restore peace and prosperity to the war torn area, where people remained divided in sympathies for either the Confederate or Union causes. William contributed both land and materials for a building to be used as both a church and a school in the valley. Like many of the churches and schools, he insisted that it be called "Union church" because it was open to all denominations and beliefs.

William died May 2, 1891 and was buried next to his parents in what was to become the Ferguson Valley Cemetery. On his tombstone, is the inscription provided by his son John Wesley, "A kind father and a true patriot".

The Cox family moved into the valley just east of Ferguson valley. It is possible they were related to or close friends of the Ferguson's since both families followed the same path from Tennessee, Missouri, War Eagle, Arkansas and then into Cox Valley within a year or two of each other. Both families found the land fertile and the location amenable and quickly settled into a life of farming and raising families. Several related families were soon to be found in the valley. These included the Bynum, Harris, Hice, Moffet, and West. The valley is still populated by many of these families. William A. Cox, married to Almira Clark in 1857, was one of the first to homestead the land. He and Almira farmed the land and raised a number of children. William wanted no part of the war, although he is thought to have sympathized with the Union cause. Bushwhackers were abundant in the region and continually raided and stole goods from the farmers. William once escaped from the bushwhackers by hiding out in the bushy outgrowth of a young walnut tree that was growing beside the house. During his lifetime, he viewed the tree as a symbol of his good luck refused to cut it from his yard.

Other relatives in the valley were not so lucky. Twenty-two year old James Kendrick and several other of the local men joined the Booneville Rifles of the 2nd Arkansas Mounted Rifles in July of 1861. They were immediately shipped to Missouri to fight at the battle of Wilson's Creek in August of that year. After the battle of Pea Ridge in 1862, many of the group were moved to the eastern theater of the war and fought in at Chicamaugua, Kinnasaw Mountain, and other major battles in the South. A collection of family letters shows the slow deterioration in Kendrick's resolve to fight. In a letter from Benton

William Ferguson Home, late 1800's

County, Arkansas dated July 23, 1861 to his wife Rachael Samantha (Meier) Kendrick, James describes his travels and states that he will serve the South until his time is up. The letter is written for him by his brother-in-law who also sends a message to his father and mother who lived in Yell County. Subsequent letters written from the Mier family to the son indicate that James is not highly regarded by his father-in-law. Rachael's father states that he is afraid she has married a contrary boy but hopes he improves. A letter dated August of 1862, Kendrick describes going out on a scouting expedition near Huntsville with various groups of men. He mentions the hard times he encounters and also sends his wife twenty dollars. The letters also describe the family fears that war will cause the family to be dispersed with some going to live in Texas or other far off places and will never be reunited. Another of Kendrick's letters speak of his love for his wife and children. His attempt at poetry reads, " The world is (are) round and the sea is deep and I long Saurt (sweetheart) in your arms to sleep." He continues, " My pen is bad, my ink is pale, My love for you will never fail." He closes by having her to kiss the children twice for him and mentions having her move back to her place and to ask Bud for assistance for the family.

According to family history, soon after this exchange of letters, Kendrick deserted or was allowed to go home on leave. Arriving home, he found Rachael Samantha had indeed obtained help in the form of a hired hand. It is not known if this is the Bud spoken of in the letter or another man that she was able to hire. Even though his wife flatly stated that she had no relationship with the worker, James flew into a rage and killed the man. Either fearing retaliation or disgruntled with the war, Kendrick deserted and joined the local guerilla group and preyed on people, including family, throughout the region. While on the way to one of his raids, he was ambushed and killed. Local lore states that his death was at the hands of Rachael and her family. Rachael and many others mentioned in the letters remained in the valley after the war, intermarrying with various locals including the family of William Cox.

CSA General W.L. Cabell

As mentioned previously, many men from what was to become Logan County joined the Union forces as a part of the First Arkansas Infantry or the Fourth Arkansas Cavalry. Both were formed in 1863 after Union forces began to occupy the central part of the state.

It is possible that some of the men were formerly Confederate soldiers under CSA General W.L. Cabell at the Battle of Devils Backbone near Greenwood on September 1, 1863. In his report, Cabell stated:

"There was nothing to make these regiments run, except the sound of the cannon. Had they fought as troops fighting for liberty should, I would have captured the whole of the enemy's command, and gone back to Fort Smith, and driven the remainder of the enemy's force off and retaken the place."

Cabell's troops, possibly composed of conscripted men that were just looking for the opportunity to change sides, panicked and ran. In the process, they ran through their own rear guard releasing more than eighty men held prisoner by Cabell. More than one-hundred of these deserters, including three officers, took part in another battle at Dardanelle, Arkansas, just eight days later – this time on the Union side. Recent enlistees of the First Infantry and 4th Cavalry were involved in the battle at Dardanelle.

Captain of Company B, 4th Arkansas Cavalry was none other than James Laffery. Laffery, a veteran of the Mexican War and owner of extensive property near Ellsworth, participated in more than forty battles and skirmishes. He joined Union forces in 1862 and was captured by Confederates in 1862. He was paroled in February of 1863 in the United States Army, First Arkansas Infantry, was in the Fayetteville fight, and was with Gen. Blount in the actions at Fort Smith and Honey Springs. He was with Gen. Cloud, when Dardanelle was captured the first time, and was also in the Haguewood fight, where he was again captured and paroled. He was in the fight at Ozark, with Brooks on his retreat from Fayetteville, and was wounded in the knee at that place. He also had his horse shot from under him, and in the fall his leg was broken. Just prior to the Haguewood fight, he had been promoted to Captain of Company B, 4th Arkansas Cavalry but had not had time yet to join them. He remained with that unit until the end of the war, participating in several other skirmishes.

On May 16, 1864, General Jo Shelby was again on the move into the area. Traveling north from Hot Springs, he had encountered and executed several guerilla forces that were marauding through the farming areas in the various valleys of the Ouachita's. According to Edwards, the thieves were taking every provision and object they could lay hands on- including women's petticoats. Shelby captured several of the guerillas, including one named Carter who was a former Confederate who was perpetrating havoc on innocent non-combatants. Showing no mercy, he killed thirty-two of the men in a skirmish and captured seventeen others. During the rapid two-hour trial of those he captured, an elderly local woman began looking over the group. Noticing one particular skulking figure, she screeched loudly and fell to the ground, rolling right and left. When she recovered sufficiently, she identified the man as the leader of a group that had attacked her home, killed her husband and oldest son, and robbed them of everything. "Would you like to execute him yourself?" asked the commanding officer. The woman thought hard and long, " No, I can't kill him, but I can stand by and see him die as I did my husband and poor, poor boy," she replied. She was given the opportunity; Shelby executed all seventeen of them.

On the night of May 16th, Shelby's men encountered part of the Arkansas Cavalry a few miles from Dardanelle. No doubt, this group included the forces commanded by Captain Laffery. The Confederate advance guards under Captain Williams encountered the U.S. Cavalry just as it was getting dark. Both sides wildly exaggerate number of enemy, and the rule of thumb is to half numbers of enemy and those killed to get anywhere close to accurate portrayals. Edwards states that the Union Cavalry totaled one-thousand strong. The advance party of Confederates fired on the surprised Union forces that immediately retreated at full gallop back toward Dardanelle. Burrel Lasaster was a member of Confederate forces attacking the town. The Lasater family owned an extensive farm near Midway – a farm currently owned by Dana Case. They had several sons and obviously had mixed convictions concerning the war. Francis, James, and William M. Lasater (all originally from Bledsoe County, Tenn.) were members of the 4th Arkansas as well as was a cousin named Burrel. The brother to the first three was also named Burrel and he was a member of the Confederate forces. This contributed to some real problems in collection of pensions after the war.

On the night of May 16th, CSA Burrel was a part of the Cavalry CSA that was in rapid pursuit of the Cavalry USA. He was in the forefront of the battle and mounted on a good horse. Burrel states;

"When the Federals were routed, they started on a dead run for Dardanelle, the Confederates pursuing. I was riding a good horse and gained fast on them and W.M. was about the hindmost one and when I got in about fifty yards of him, I recognized him as my brother. I pushed the stronger ahead to capture him and when, in about twenty yards ahead of me, his horse stumbled and fell, throwing him over his head in the road, his left shoulder striking first as near as I could remember. I made a halt to see that our forces did not hurt him. He got up on his hands and knees and went over a bank to the right of the road and in the brush. I got the horse and saddle and carried them off with me."

Shelby occupied the town, several of the Union officers escaped by jumping into rafts and escaping down the river leaving their men behind. Shelby reports that 374 of the Union force of over 2,000 were wounded or killed in the battle for the town, excluding the number killed in the clash of the two groups of cavalry and the number who drowned trying to escape. They took 233 prisoners, including Captain James Laferry. Shelby was known to have executed others who had violated previous paroles so he must not have been aware that Laferry was again captured and released. It is possible that several other local men many have been captured since Laferry's troops included Joseph Horn, Hansel Trusty, Henry Collier, John and Samuel Foster, Newton Hibbs, George, James, and Walter Moore, James Plunket, John and William Rogers, John Widener, Levander Sikes, and others. All Union company records, equipment, muster rolls, and property were lost.

Shelby wished to attack Norristown (Russellville) as well but upon learning of a deadly measles epidemic there, he and his men moved back into the mountains of central Arkansas.

Dardanelle was a hotbed of activity during the Civil War. Steamboats could navigate the Arkansas River to Dardanelle year round and the Military road passed through the town on its way into Oklahoma. Prior to the war, the Butterfield stage passed through Dardanelle with stops at Pottsville, Stinnets Station, Paris, Charleston, and Lavaca before joining the northern route that entered Fort Smith from Van Buren and northward. After the capture of Fort Smith in August of 1863, Union forces established supply lines from overland from Kansas and by boat up the Arkansas from the Mississippi River. During dry seasons, steamboats would land in Dardanelle and offload goods onto freight wagons which would then travel overland into Fort Smith. Large contingents of Union troops were placed in Dardanelle to protect these goods. Smaller groups of Union troops scouted out of redoubts built at Clarksville, Roseville, Ozark,

Hot Springs during 1850's

and other small towns. These troops also tried, with limited success, to protect a telegraph line that ran from Little Rock to Fort Smith.

Confederate forces attacked every supply line possible and were constantly cutting the telegraph line and bushwhacking groups sent to repair it. Dardanelle was repeatedly attacked and counter-attacked during the last two years of the war and groups skirmished daily throughout the region.

The largest expedition during the latter part of the war involved General Steele's attack on Southern Arkansas and the Confederate forces in Camden in April of 1864. Fourteen thousand union troops from across the state converged on forces commanded by General Fagan, Shelby, Cabell, and others. Union troops were pulled out of Fort Smith to join the battle. Pvt. Henry Strong of Company K, 12th Kansas Infantry was one of the men forced to march south for the battle. His journey is described in an interesting personnel diary that provides insight about the River Valley. Travelling east from Fort Smith on the Old Military road, he observes a mountain near Charleston which he called "tater hill," a name it retains today. His troop bogged through terrible weather and worse roads, turning at Charleston and proceeding through Chismville. At Chismville, it is possible he stopped at the home of William Wayne Williams and his family. Williams and his eight children were on their way to Texas in an attempt to avoid the problems created by the Civil War in Tennessee. Traveling in an ox cart loaded with supplies and children, they attempted to cross six-mile creek near Chismville. The oxen became frightened by loose horses and plunged into a large rock in the creek. Twelve year old John Williams and fourteen year old sister Nancy were seriously injured. Unable to continue, the family leased the Chism house from Ben Chism who had recently married one of the Titsworth girls and moved to Roseville.

Chismville was a significant town, located at the junction of several roads and a mail station. It eventually grew to a community of close to two-thousand people and remained one of the most important towns in the county until eventually being supplanted by the development of a rail station in Booneville.

Chismville, Early 1900's

The two-storied cabin where the Williams (and Chism's) resided in now being restored and is an Arkansas Historical site .

Pvt. Strong has little to say about Chismville but his description of Booneville is far from complementary- referring to it as a small collection of smoke-covered hovels. From Booneville, the group traveled through Danville, thus to Hot Springs, and to their eventual inglorious defeat at Poison Springs, Marks Mill, and Camden.

With the Union defeat in South Arkansas, Confederate troops again aggressively moved through the River Valley. Small skirmishes occurred throughout the mountain region with several battles occurring at Waldron, Charleston, Booneville, Clarksville, and Ozark.

Thousands of refugees felt they had no alternative except to emigrate to the North. They could not live in safety outside of the military posts, and starvation faced them within the posts. On August 8, 1864 a refugee train of about 1,500 people, the largest up to that time, left Fort Smith for the northwest states. Although thousands left northwest Arkansas during 1864 for the North, several thousand refugees still remained who were dependent upon the United States government for support. It was estimated in March 1865, from the official returns of rations issued, that almost as many rations were issued to refugees as to Union troops in Fort Smith, Van Buren and Fayetteville. Union officials began to collect groups of individuals and to place them in one location on farming plantations. More the two-dozen of these plantations existed across northwest Arkansas affording individual's mutual protection and a farm on which to live. Atrocities that compare to those carried out by Islamic radicals were committed throughout the Arkansas River Valley, especially during the last year and a half of the war. Many of the reported atrocities were committed by Union troops upon the people they were supposed be guarding. A group of five or six Union soldiers raided the home of Mrs. Lutetia Howell and her sister-in-law Susan Willis of Johnson County. Thinking she had hidden money, they threatened her with her life. When she still refused to provide information about buried gold, they stripped her right foot and thrust it into the hot coals of the fireplace. The leg was burned so badly that the flesh fell off her leg from knee to toe. Mrs. Willis was also given the same treatment but refused to talk. They were both thrown into a deserted slave quarters where they applied linseed oil to their burns. The men burned the house to the ground before they left the next morning. Fourteen other area homes were burned to the ground. Five other women in the community received similar treatment and Mrs. O. Wallis and Mrs. Wiley Harris were whipped to the point of death. One of the men who reported the incident described the torture as to horrible to place in print. W.S. Jetton described the hanging and murder of Daniel Farmer, his fifteen year son, and 85 year old man Jetton. The women could not obtain a coffin for Mr. Jetton and ended digging a grave the best they could and burying him in a home-made quilt. Children had to grow up early- two twelve year old relatives had to come and get Mr. Farmer and his son, place their bodies on an ox cart, and carry them over to Clarksville to be buried. Similar atrocities occurred throughout the area. Although arrests were made in the case, it appears that none of the individuals ever received any punishment other than temporary imprisonment. Near Blue Ball, a Union soldier with evil intention burst into the Millard household. The frightened woman was able to not only escape but shot and killed her assailant as well. Fearful of retribution, the soldier was buried in a shallow unmarked grave in the Millard yard.

Similar stories occurred throughout the region and hundreds fled the area. Is seems that families on the benches and ridges of Magazine Mountain were better prepared and more organized in

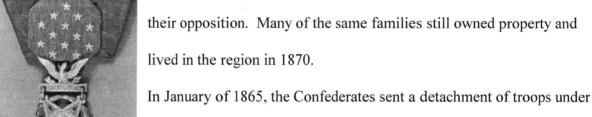

their opposition. Many of the same families still owned property and lived in the region in 1870.

In January of 1865, the Confederates sent a detachment of troops under Colonel William H. Brooks to harass Union steamboats traveling on the Arkansas River between Little Rock and Fort Smith. To counter this force, Colonel Abraham Ryan sent Major James Jenks and 276 men to occupy Dardanelle and to prevent attacks from the Confederates. The battle was intense and lasted more than four hours before the South withdrew. During this battle, Union Sergeant William Ellis of the Third Wisconsin Cavalry received Arkansas first Congressional Medal of Honor for his valor and bravery above and beyond the call of duty

Ellis enlisted in the Union Army at Little Rock, Arkansas. He is representative of the large

number of Arkansans (one Arkansan in five who fought in the

war did so wearing the Union blue) who did not favor secession

and the disruption of the United States.

Leaving Dardanelle, Brooks headed west in pursuit of Union

steamboats. He established an ambush on the south side of the

river at Ivey's ford near Roseville. A flotilla of steamers

including the *Admiral Hines*, the *Lotus*, the *Anne Jacobs*, and the

New Chippewa had completed a mission of delivering supplies

to Fort Smith and were on their way back downstream. The boats, under the command of

Colonel Thomas Bowen of the 13th Kansas, included a small contingent of troops from several

units as well as some Union refugees.

At about one o'clock in the afternoon of January 17, the *New Chippewa* approached the

Confederate position at Ivey's Ford and was immediately raked with artillery and rifle fire. The

steamboat attempted to escape but ran aground on the south bank. Brooks men captured about

thirty men of the 15th Indiana as well as some union refugees. Everything of value was taken

from the boat and it was set on fire. The *Annie Jacobs* and the *Lotus* were hammered by artillery

as they passed the Confederate stronghold and both grounded on the north bank of the river.

Bowen gathered the men around him and sent word to the Admiral Jacobs to prevent it running

into the trap. Twenty-seven Union soldiers were killed and more than eighty were captured.

With news of Union re-enforcements, the Confederate troops broke off the attack and retreated

southward. The Annie Jacobs was abandoned and the other ships continued downriver.

Stories abound concerning lost treasure from the Union ships which were supposedly carrying payroll downstream. When attacked, the steamer captain locked the safe and deposited it overboard, buried in the sands of the river. Although several cannon ball and artifacts have been discovered, the treasure, if it existed, still remains buried beneath the river.

The actions at Dardanelle and Ivey's Ford marked the last serious Confederate attempts to challenge Union control of the Arkansas River. Though both sides continued to make periodic scouts and raids into enemy territory, no other serious combat operations occurred in Arkansas during the remainder of the Civil War.

The battle of Appomattox Court House, fought April 9, 1865, ended with the surrender of Generals Lee's forces to General U.S. Grant. Confederates across the South began to accept defeat, turn in arms, and

Bushwhakers Hideout, Huckleberry Mt.

return to their homes. Arkansas, a prosperous state prior to the war, was destitute. As the various groups drifted back to their homes, they found abandoned villages, burned-out buildings, and farm returned to wilderness. Family members were scattered and communication links between them were non-existent. Neighbors with differing political views and affiliations looked upon each other with mistrust and sometimes downright hatred. People with Southern ties were stripped of the right to vote and citizenship for a period of ten years. Federal troops were stationed throughout the state to enforce law and maintain peace. The South was a conquered land- one badly in need or healing.

To Heal a Savage Land

The most amazing thing about the Civil War is not that it occurred or the severity of it but the fact that within a short period of time, men who had bleed hatred and pure violence could pull back together into one unified people. Although it probably seemed a lifetime to those living through that period of time, within ten years states that had tried to separate into an independent nation were again recognized as equal partners within a growing United States of America. In fact, Arkansas had already elected a new governor and established state government before the war was even complete. Men that had fought for their individual rights were again practicing the civil liberties guaranteed to them by a Constitution they had denounced. As armies began to dissolve, former soldiers began to trickle back to their home. Those fighting for the South had to renounce the Confederacy and swear oaths to the federal government. Many of the men signed official papers of surrender before leaving their units- other simply deserted and headed home. One out of five Arkansas men that was involved in the war fought for the Union. For them, the transition was easier and they returned home ready and able to participate in the post-war changes that were taking place in the South.

Those with Confederate ties found it much more difficult. Not only were they stripped of voting privileges, they returned home to a land that was vastly different from when they left. Those that had invested heavily in the plantation system found that their property was destroyed, their family scattered, and their structure of making a living through a system based on slavery no longer existed. Prior to the war, large sums of money had been invested in obtaining labor through the purchase of fellow humans at an average cost of more than $1,000 per slave. Returning to a war ravaged land, the plantation owners found they had no credit, no labor to work the land, and were deep in debt with unpaid bills and taxes. Former slaves and poor whites were often just as destitute. Lacking capital, the region was plunged into a system of sharecropping, tenant farming, or mere subsistence- all three problems which would plague Arkansas and the people of the River Valley for years to come. Adding to the problem, many carpetbaggers and other adventurers moved into the region and preyed on a defeated people. An examination of the lives of those from the shadow of the mountains allows us to trace the changes that were going on in our region and in the United States.

Captain James Lafferry and James Garner survived Haguewood Prairie and the rest of the war. Lafferry, married to Martha (Smith) Lafferry in 1852, had nine children prior to the war. A native of Hamilton County, Tennessee, the Captain owned more than 350 acres of land that he had purchased when he arrived in Arkansas in 1858. Fifty of those acres were under cultivation near the community of Ellsworth and that is where is home was located. Martha Smith was also a

Martha E. (Lafferry) Smith, Mcneal, Cravens (1870's)

native of Hamilton County and her father, Reuben, had followed James to Arkansas and settled near Scranton. Mary had eight siblings and many relatives including the Spicer, Walker, and Wheeler's. Captain Laffery's brother George also moved into the area around Scranton. He married Elizabeth Pridgen and one of their daughters was Martha E. Lafferry. She is of interest since she eventually marries and outlives three husbands, (1) Josiah A. Smith, (2) William Leonard McNeal, and (3) Jerry Cravens, that were well known during the early history of Logan County. Another of James's niece married into the Plunkett family and many descendants of these families still reside in the county.

Lafferry immediately returned to a life of farming and producing children- he eventually fathered thirteen offspring. He was appointed United States receiver in the land office at Dardanelle by

E.J., Wesley, Caroline, Jack, Martha, Huey, Mahalia, and Ethel (Lafferry) Plunket in 1889.

President Grant in 1873. That the appointment was a political plum is evident in the fact that James Shrigley, another of Lafferry's war companions, was mentioned in the same article in the *New York Times* as being appointed as land register for Dardanelle. Lafferry was also appointed to appraise the land at what was then called the Fort Smith Reservation.

In 1871, the state legislature determined that it would be more cost effective and practical to increase the number of counties. The area now known as Logan County was carved from Franklin, Scott, Johnson, and Yell and was first named Sarber after a carpetbagging State Senator from Yell County named John Sarber. James Garner, C.P. Anderson, and James L. White were appointed commissioners to set up the County Seat. Instructions were to set the County Seat near the center of the newly formed county and to set it up in an assessable site. There were only three major roads in the county at that time- Military Road, a road running from Booneville to Dardanelle along present day Hwy 10, and what was known as Booneville road which ran from Morrison Bluff, over Red Bench, and into Booneville. The temporary county seat of justice was set up at Reveille. At that time, Reveille was located on Red Bench Road about a mile east of today's Hwy 309. It has several businesses, a post office, and was located near the grist mill owned by James Garner. A court house and jail was built and the small town was called Anderson.

A year later, a new set of commissioners were appointed. These included James Lafferry, Daniel E. Lee, and James Shrigley. This group raised the ire of the entire county by moving the County Seat to Ellsworth. Ellsworth was a thriving community consisting of several businesses, post office, and a large Methodist Church. All three of the men owned property and businesses in the area. People across the county were incensed by the commission's actions and rumors of financial impropriety and shoddy workmanship on the new Court House soon had the county inhabitants literally up in arms. Feelings ran strong and armed men threatened to intervene. The court house caught on fire and burned to the ground, destroying many of the early county records.

James Logan

In 1873, the same group of men voted to establish a new and permanent county seat in a small village near Short Mountain creek. A court house was built and the town that would become Paris was established.

In 1875, the right to vote was given back to the men who fought for the Confederacy. Most of these men were ardently opposed to many of the laws passed by the Reconstruction era politicians. They joined the Democratic Party in mass and quickly gained control of state and local government. Opposed to anything enacted by the Reconstruction government, they quickly changed the name of the county from Sarber to Logan, named for James Logan, one of the founding fathers of the county.

Lafferry was very involved in county politics throughout his life. He proved to be a very successful farmer and business man. During his lifetime, he acquired land in Yell County, near Baxter cemetery in Paris, and even substantial property in California. He established a strong Grand Army of the Republic (GAR) post at Ellsworth and was known as a strong benefactor and member of the Methodist Episcopal Church. In 1889, <u>The Biographical and Historical Memoirs</u> <u>of Western Arkansas</u> name him as one of the most prominent members of the county. He died in November of 1895 and is buried in Ellsworth Cemetery.

The life of James L. Garner and Lafferry often appear intertwined. Both originated in the same part of the county, had fought in the Mexican War, moved to Arkansas, and fought in both the 1st Arkansas Infantry and as officers in the 4th Arkansas Cavalry. James owned property and farmed on Red Bench road. He also ran the grist mill at Mill Pond on Cove Creek and after the war, was very involved in local politics. James L. withdrew from military service in 1864 while serving as a lieutenant in the 4th Cavalry. At the time, he was suffering from an illness, possibly the result of an inoculation given to the Arkansas troops at Ft. Smith. The inoculation resulted in serious illness for several of the troops and resulted in some deaths.

Prior to the war, James L. had travelled to California to join the gold rush. When the train master deserted them, James was elected as train master and was able to get the wagons safely to California. He was successful enough to bring back a small pot of gold. While he was away during the war, the rumors of wealth resulted in a visit by bushwhackers who forced his wife to reveal the hiding place of the remaining gold. The bushwhackers stole the gold and most of the family livestock. When James returned, his wife revealed that she knew the identity of some of the bushwhackers and James was able to track them down. He recovered much of the stolen livestock but the gold had already been spent.

James L. was a close relative of Benjamin Wilkins who was killed at the battle of Haguewood Prairie. Benjamin's wife was left with seven small children. She died soon after the war and James L. received guardianship of the three of the younger children.

James served as a Justice of the Peace for his township and was eventually elected to serve in the state legislature in 1872. He was instrumental in getting Logan County carved from the surrounding counties and it setting up the first county seat.

James L. was a colorful character. When he was a young lad, he and his family lived near Davy Crockett and much admired the man, so much so that he named one of his son's Crockett. He also became adopted the convention of wearing a coon skin cap. Attracted to rattlesnakes, he would sit out on the bluff near his homes and observe them in the rocks below. After capturing some of the larger specimen, he made himself a vest and belt of the skin. A tall, dark, imposing man, he cut quite a figure when he stood to speak in the state legislature dressed out in his frontier garb.

After serving in the legislature, he returned home and was appointed the first Sherriff of Logan County. He was then elected to the position and served out another term in the turbulent years following the War. Whether due to living life with the candle burning at both ends or because of illness resulting from his war experiences, James died an early death at the age of fifty-one years.

The Lee family is one of the largest and oldest families in the region. William and Dicey Lee built a log cabin near Paint Rock in 1837. By the time the Civil War began, his offspring owned property across the county. His grandson George, son of Britton Lee, was the first person buried at Paint Rock Cemetery. In 1862, the young ten-year old boy was helping cut wood when a large oak tree fell on him, crushing him to death. All of the family was known to be ardent Union supporters so

Colonel John Griffith of 17th AR.

the war was very difficult for them. Most of the family fled to the safety of Fort Smith to escape bushwhackers. As recorded in earlier chapters, Daniel and Thomas Lee survived their ordeal at Haguewood Prarie. Daniel lived for thirty years after the war, spending many of his later years with Thomas who had established his home in the town of Millard.

Thomas Lee married Martha Jane Moore in October of 1870. Martha was one of a number of children of John Moore of Greasy Valley. Thomas's relative, James K. Lee, another member of the 1st Arkansas Infantry had married her older sister Arminta. James and Arminta, lived on a farm just south of the Subiaco City lake. They were the parents of Pike Lee and ten other children. Thomas and Martha had eight children who married into the Rogers, Fink, Zeiler, and other families of the Mountain. *The Paris Express* obituary of March 19, 1925 states that pioneer citizen Thomas A. Lee died near Millard community on March 13 of that year and was buried at Moore Cemetery in Greasy valley.

Benjamin B. Chism, one of the first to leave the county and join the Confederate cause, was the son of Jeanetta Logan (daughter of Colonel James Logan), and a son-in-law of the prominent Titsworth family. At the age of sixteen, he enlisted with Captain J.R. Titsworth's 5th Arkansas Infantry (CSA) and fought at the battle of Oak Hill and later at Pea Ridge. He was moved over to the 17th Arkansas Infantry and served with Captain David Arbuckle. After Arbuckle was captured, eighteen year old Benjamin served as company commander. He then served as Aide-de-Camp for Colonel John Griffith and was commended for his reconnaissance and capture of the Federal gunboat Petrel on the Yazoo River. Even though a former Confederate, in 1874 he was elected

General John Marmaduke

Delegate to the Constitutional Convention and also commissioned a Colonel of Militia by Governor Baxter. In 1876 he was elected State Senator for the counties of Yell and Logan. In 1888 he was elected Secretary of State for the two years from 1889 to 1891. He lived his out his later years in the county seat at Paris.

It is strange that many of the men who fought for the Confederacy eventually not only returned to the Union but also became important officials in the government. General John Marmaduke, commander of Jo Shelby and the CSA troops at Haguewood, was captured in Missouri late in the war. He spent some time in Federal prison before being released at the conclusion of the war. Marmaduke went on to serve as Governor of the state of Missouri.

General Jo Shelby, Confederate commander at the battle of Haguewood Prairie and hero of the famous Missouri raid, returned to Arkadelphia in October, 1864 celebrated as one of the most renowned cavalry leaders of the Civil War. When the war was complete, he and his men refused to surrender, traveling to Mexico instead. His trip is legendary- a true to life western that was eventually made into the movie, *The Undefeated,* starring none other than John Wayne and Rock Hudson. His aide-to-camp, John Edwards, became a newspaper editor in Kansas City and was responsible for developing the legends surrounding the life of Frank and Jessie James. Shelby's friend and aide, Col. Alonzo Slayback, famous for his individual duel on horseback during the battle of Prairie Grove, accompanied Shelby and his troops into Mexico. He later became a prominent leader in the St. Louis bar association. He became involved in a public political argument with the editor of the

St. Louis Post Dispatch. When Slayback confronted the editor John Cockerill, the man pulled a revolver from his pocket and killed Slayback, thus ended the life of one of the bravest and most remarkable men to have fought in the Civil War.

Shelby eventually returned to Missouri, received a pardon, and was appointed by President Grant to be the post of U.S. Marshall. While serving in that capacity, he provided a character reference for Frank James at his famous trial for lawlessness.

Color guard, Dedication of Haguewood Prairie Monument

September 27, 2013 marked the sesquicentennial of the battle of Haguewood Prairie. More than sixty students from surrounding communities filmed a reenactment of the battle and over twenty-five hundred people attended the dedication and reenactment of the battle during Frontier Days, 2013. Civil War re-enactors from the 13th Arkansas (CSA), Dardanelle Flag Corp (10th CSA), Arkansas 1st Infantry, Old Fort Smith (U.S.), Drennan House Museum (Van Buren), and North Logan County Museum participated in the dedication, firing of Civil War armament, and frontier crafts and games demonstration.

The monument and historical marker were presented, not to remind inhabitants of the war, but to remind us of our historical roots and of man's ability to persevere and work through great hardships. Before the turn of the 19th century, the bitter, angry opponents that had survived the war began to meet in friendly reunions around the United States. President U.S. Grant visited Little Rock and was paraded down Main Street. While a sense of unity was present, Southern pride was evident and ran deep. The 1911 national Confederate reunion was held in Little Rock and attracted 140,000 people and as many as 20,000 veterans. It was the single largest event in

Little Rock history prior to the inauguration of President Bill Clinton. Logan County, with several Grand Army of the Republic (GAR) and United Confederate Veterans (UCV) organizations, had several delegates at the meeting. Thousands of people lined Main Street, Little Rock as the veterans marched twenty-two decorated blocks in the May heat. The reunion was again held in Little Rock in 1928. One of the telling photos from that reunion displays two old men, one in blue, the other gray, arms outstretched around the other's shoulders and a smile on their faces. The epitaph on the Paris monument contains the following statement:

No North or South, or East or West, WE ARE ONE!!!

Ridge Runners and Valley People

Although Logan County has a diversity of people, the people of the ridges and valleys are predominately of Scotch-Irish background. Scotch-Irish tends to be a generic name applied to groups of people- primarily Presbyterian- that migrated to America during its early history. Originally they referred to themselves as Irish but, added the qualifier Scotch later to distinguish themselves from the Irish Catholics who arrived after the potato famines of the 18th century. Many of this group had migrated to Northern Ireland from various parts of the British Empire, including part of Holland, and had been used by the British king to fight against the Irish insurgencies that swept the country. A hardy stock of people, they tended to seek out the less desirable rocky and steep hillsides of the Appalachian Mountains. They were no stranger to the hardships, poverty, and frontier battles that awaited them. The term hillbilly, with its connotations of poverty, backwardness, and violence; is often applied to the group and their descendants.

The Scotch-Irish migration to and through America involves networks of related families who settle together, worship together, and often intermarried. They often refer to their group as "clans" and are "clannish" to the exclusion of others. In the various communities located along the River Valley, one is often first referred to by family name first and outsiders are identified by

River Raft, unknown artist

what family they "married" into. Common statements might sound something like, "Yeah, that gal moved in here from Fort Smith and married into the Varnell family." Even after years of living in a community, the person is still identified by the town from which they arrived and by the family into which they married.

The Scotch-Irish in the River Valley follows the general settlement patterns described above. Most of Arkansas earlier settlers came from surrounding states- especially Tennessee. The slopes and ridges of Magazine Mountain are inhabited by large groups of families from Hamilton and Bledsoe County in eastern Tennessee. It looks like entire neighborhoods of people were scooped up and transported bodily to Logan and Yell County Arkansas and dropped them into communities. More likely, a small number migrated up the Cumberland River, down the Ohio and Mississippi, and up the Arkansas on john boats and started small communities. Communications back home would describe the advantages of Arkansas, especially those that would attract the footloose Scotch-Irish. Cheap land, wild game to hunt, great climate, and best of all, little governmental control and regulation probably sounded like a dream come true to people suffering through the various bank failures and economic depressions that hit the U.S. during the 1830's.

Former U.S. Senator James Webb does an exceptional job of describing the character of the Scotch-Irish. In his book, *Born Fighting*, he describes the history of the group and ascribes general character traits found in the population.

Those traits include loyalty to kin, extreme mistrust in governmental authority and legal systems, and a propensity to bear arms and to know how to use them. In addition, one could probably add several other that appear to be common denominators. Like most ethnic groups, the Scotch- Irish have common foods, religious

96

beliefs and practices, funeral rituals, superstitions, music, and other practices. Growing up in the hollows and benches, one does not realize the uniqueness of culture of the region.

Relatives within the community are referred to as kinfolk. This extended group might go back several generations and include third, fourth, and even fifth cousins. Some people living in the community are called almost kin- meaning family relationships go back so many years that they share common blood from generations extending back more than a century. In Midway, the Miller family are almost kin to the Varnell's. Settie Miller was originally a Case and shared a common ancestor with the Varnell clan- as a result; Rickey Miller is *almost kin* to me. In-fighting within families or kin was sometimes common but, if provoked at school or on the bus by an outside family, one might find themselves at war with an entire group.

Spiro, Oklahoma was introduced to this cultural aspect during the 1968 Arkansas-Oklahoma State fair held in Fort Smith. Paris had about thirty students participating in the various judging contest and competitions. Most of us were not nearly as interested in judging cattle or pigs as we were in getting out of school for a day and playing at the carnival.

During the day, one of the younger Paris students won a large stuffed bear only to have it stolen by a much larger and older Spiro student. After stealing the bear, he left it in his bus only to have it stolen back by Paris students assisting the young man from whom it was stolen.

By the time the group of students I was with arrived back at the bus, Spiro had rounded up three busloads of students and descended upon the few Paris students in the bus. One of the largest Spiro kids, spoiling for a fight, had thrown his hat onto the ground and daring anyone from Paris to step on it. Herbert Howard, all six foot and hundred ten pounds of him, was working up the courage to get himself squashed by a guy a hundred pounds heavier and three years older than himself. Vastly outnumbered and outsized, most of we Paris kids were shuffling our feet and edging our way out of the conflict. Seeing or predicament, Scranton tumbled out of their bus with Chuck Hughes in the forefront. Without hesitation, he smashed the hat and the fight was on. County Line and Dardanelle poured out of their various buses and the border war began in earnest. Determined to assist but not being raised a fool by my parents, I began to look for me a four foot tall Spiro pygmy. Although there wasn't one in sight, I circled the group valiantly looking tough and trying to maintain my honor. Country kids were exchanging blows and rolling across the turf around the bus and Spiro was looking for a way to extract themselves from a mad group of hillbillies. Fortunately for them, the agriculture teachers saw what was going on and came running up the hill. Paris agriculture teacher at that time was Mr. James Morris. For obvious reasons, he was known affectionately as *Chrome Dome* by all of his students. As soon as he saw the melee, he began running at this top speed up the hill- tufts of hair above each ear flying in the wind, screaming at the top of his voice for us to stop. Not having found a worthy (and small enough) opponent, stopping was easy for me. For others, it was a more strenuous and difficult task of extraction. The large kid from Spiro was spinning round and round in a tight circle, one Paris kid with a death grip around his neck from behind, one holding onto his legs, and with blood pouring from a nose that Chuck has dotted. As soon as the kids released him, he used his football speed to extract himself back to the safety of the Spiro bus. Just another lesson in "we might pick on each other, but you better leave kinfolk alone!!!!"

Until funeral homes recently enacted certain rules concerning days and times for burial, the people of the mountain had a unique and prescribed pattern of burial.

When a person became seriously ill, all family members are called in for a period of "setting up." Since there were few hospitals, most of the time this occurred in the home. Uncle Roy Moore was seriously ill with cancer and his chances of recovery were slim. Brothers, sisters, nephew, cousins, and other blood relatives were alerted and all made their way to his home to pay respects and to "sit up." No self-respecting family would allow their loved ones to die without family members being present- no matter time of day or night. If the person lingered on for a period of time, family members took turns sitting up. Children, like myself at the time, would make pallets and sleep on the floor or even outside on the porch. Being superstitious, people would watch for signs that death was imminent. This could include a rooster crowing in the middle of the night, dogs or wolves barking repeatedly, or unexpected night sounds such as bells, turtle dove cooing, or the miss striking of a clock. During an extended illness, one never swept under the bed or moved the person from one bed to another. All were signs of bad luck. Until the early 1900's, most people were not embalmed. When the person passed away, the body was prepared for the funeral. This usually began an extended period of sitting up and mourning together. The deceased was placed in the coffin and brought back to their home. When my uncle Russell Varnell died at age thirty-six, my grandmother had his body brought to her house for the traditional three day waiting period. The casket was opened and placed in the

Reverand Gorman Daniel speaking at Hickory Groove Decoration Day

living room. Chairs packed the room and family and friends gathered day and night to remember his life. Every neighbor within miles brought in food for the family. All work, cooking, cleaning, everything shut down for that period of time. Everyone within a community attends funerals. In fact, some within the community go to all funerals in the area regardless of family affiliation. For some of the elderly, funerals can be a time of gathering, seeing people from the surrounding area, and just visiting with those lucky enough to still be alive.

Cemeteries dot the mountainsides of the River Valley. Some contain only family plots while others contain dozens of related families. Each year during May, each cemetery has an unofficial holiday called "decoration" where family members bring flowers and tokens of remembrance and place on the graves as a sign of respect and love for those who have passed. Grandma Nettie Varnell and other women would spend days making paper carnations and roses to place on all of the graves at Hickory Groove cemetery in St. Louis Valley. Later, as the family became more financially able, sprays and arrangements were bought and live flower were planted on sites to remember the family.

Decoration Day brought family in from across several states. Family members would begin meeting right after daylight on the designated Sunday and would place flowers on the graves. Afterward, members of the extended family would visit until the minister arrived and delivered the sermon. Since many families have relatives buried in various cemeteries; the hill people, by custom, have arranged decoration on set Sundays during the month of May.

For more than forty years, Reverend Gorman Daniel of Midway would dismiss his church early and then preach sermons on successive Sundays at Horne, Hickory Groove, and Ellsworth Cemeteries. At Hickory Groove, children would play in the old church house and at the bottom of the hill while family placed flower arrangements on the graves. To allow children or adults to step on the grave sites was not only disrespectful but, according to superstition, would result in the soon death of a family member. The only counter to the curse was to jump backwards across it right away. Since I had enough trouble jumping forward, the thought of accidently stepping on a grave brought me nightmares.

There are several other superstitions associated with burial. One is if the person digging the grave is not present to watch the funeral and to see it refilled, they are marked for early death. How many funerals have you attended and observed the grave crew waiting to refill the site? Now you know the rest of the story. It is also generally believed that bad luck and death occurs in groups of three and that it is bad luck for a funeral procession to stop on the way to the cemetery. Answers a lot of questions including why processions are preceded by police cars and people not in the procession are expected to vacate right of way.

Most of the Varnell family eventually sold used cars. As such, they were self-employed and were available to serve as pall-bearers without missing valuable work time. My father and various uncles served in this capacity on so many occasions, they knew every funeral home director and employee in two or three counties. Since they were so readily available and had a hard time declining assistance to a family in need, they often became involved in funerals of people that were relatives of friends of friends. As such, they often had to be introduced to the family members whom they were assisting. At one such funeral, my youngest uncle Danny was assisting in the burial of a rather heavy recently deceased lady. The six pall-bearers were finding it a difficult task disembarking the coffin from the hearse and proceeding up the wet slippery red clay hill of the cemetery. Slipping and sliding, they placed the coffin upon the metal platform located directly above the grave. Danny stumbled as he walked the coffin onto the platform. As he sought to gain his balance, his right foot slipped into the grave. Startled, a look of terror flashed across his face as he disappeared into the hole beneath the coffin. Upon reaching the bottom of the red clay hole, panic ensued and Danny tried to extricate himself by climbing the shear walls. With help from family and pall bearers, he was freed from the gummy clay. Dark red smears covered his light blue suit, his hands, and even his face. The oft repeated tale of his extraction and subsequent embarrassment still circulates throughout the community.

Mountain people tell spooky tales of supernatural, unnatural, and just plain spooky. Raised on those tales, it is easy to believe in the appearance of angels, ghosts, and even of visits from the spirits. Most families have at least two or three such experiences that they like to describe, thoughts of which fill a young heads with terror and keep one from wondering to far afield while out in the neighborhood at night.

In 1974, my father purchased a used fully-equipped Cadillac hearse. Complete with curtains, rollers in the floor, and sliding partition behind the front seat, it had everything a mortician wanted in a vehicle.

Borrowing it from my dad, I drove it to Mockingbird Hill to the home of the most superstitious person I knew, my boss Jack Hatcher. While going home one evening, a black cat ran across 109 highway in front of Jacks car. Skidding to a stop, he drove back to Subiaco, east on highway 22, over to Prairie View, and home- a trip six miles out of his way. Figuring on creating excitement in his home, I backed the hearse up to his front door and honked the horn.

Curtis and Curtis James Varnell

Immediately, every neighbor within two miles began calling to check out the situation. I worked with Jack for about three more years and, by the conclusion of that period of time, he could finally see the humor in my prank.

Dad sold the vehicle to one of the Johns family. The youngest son in the family drove it to Paris high school and organized a funeral procession through Paris during the lunch hour. Twenty or more vehicles lined up behind the hearse as the backed out of the school parking area. All twenty followed the hearse down North 10th with their lights on. Much to the delight of the students, cars began to pull over the curb, the mailman stood to attention and took off his hat, and the kids waved with excitement out the windows of the packed hearse. Proceeding through town without stopping at any light, the procession turned south and headed to the Eagle, a restaurant located near Short Mountain Creek. As they began to unload, several police cars with flashing red lights pulled in behind the crowd. According to local rumor, the owner was offered a deal he could not refuse- sale of the vehicle or a ticket exceeding several hundred dollars. The incident marked the demise and departure of the hearse from the City of Paris.

Many other superstitions and myths abound throughout the region. My father was the third of ten boys born to Lee and Nettie (Moore) Varnell. All except Danny, the youngest, was delivered by a midwife. In Midway, Sadie Crowell served as the midwife and delivered most of the children. When my father was delivered, Aunt Sadie took my grandmother aside and told her dad was marked for a special life. He was born with a veil (caul). A caul is a piece of membrane that covers a newborn's head and face. It is harmless and is usually removed immediately by the doctor or midwife. Many famous people including Sigmund Freud, Charlemagne, Napoleon and others were born under the vale. Children born with such a veil expect long lives full of good luck and extraordinary powers. Cauls occur in about one out of every 800,000 births. The truly superstitious believe that a caul birth allows one to predict events, to commune with the deceased, and to have extraordinary perception.

Although unsure of the other traits, dad has an extraordinary ability to deal with other people. This has been of great benefit to him in doing business and knowing when to make important decisions. He has also been very successful in doing whatever he wished in life. Rising from a very humble beginning, he developed an extensive business relationship with car companies and dealers in several states. In later years, he was able to purchase the house and business he always wanted to own. He retired early enough that he and my mother were able to travel extensively and develop his hobby of buying antiques, especially clocks.

Family history indicates that men in the Varnell family have a propensity to develop heart problems at an early age and to have shortened life spans. My grandfather died in his early forties as did many of my uncles. Dad has lived in excess of eighty years and still enjoys life enough to keep the roads "hot" between Paris and Russellville. Caul, hard work, clean living, or just luck- we are fortunate that Aunt Sadie predictions have come true.

William, my oldest uncle, was born without an ear. My grandmother always believed that she "marked" him while he was in the womb. My grandfather had killed several squirrels and my grandmother was cleaning them. While doing so, she pulled her hair back leaving a bloody streak over her ear. When William was born, no ear flap existed on that side. My mother always laughed about such superstitions until her daughter-in-law was seen assisting her dog deliver puppies while pregnant with her grandchild. Screaming frantically, she grabbed the daughter-in-law and forced her away from the animal. Superstitions do not easily die.

Nettie and William Varnell, note the absence of the right ear!

One of the strangest superstitions or believes of the region concerns the mad stone. The mad stone is a stony concretion taken from the stomach of an albino deer. The common description is that is slightly oval and measures about three or four inches in circumference.

Mad Stone, National Museum of Health and Medicine, Washington, D.C.

The mad stone, when used correctly, has curative powers. Mad stones have said to have the ability to cure rabies, rattlesnake, and spider bites among other things. Several people, including the Cox family, have owned and used mad stones in this region. Velma Ezell of the Mount Salem community describes a relative using the stone and following a strict set of rules in order for it to work. One of the primary regulations is that there is to never be a charge for its services. It is freely provided to those desperate for its use. It was usually passed from father to son and used for generations.

When needed, the stone is place upon the wound or bite. The wound must be fresh and bleeding, if it isn't, the skin is scraped until bleeding. The stone is placed directly upon the wound and will stick to the wound if the infection is present. It is left attached until it falls from the wound. At that time, it is boiled in sweet milk until the milk turns green, indicating that the poison is pulled from the wound. The stone is then removed from the milk and the procedure is repeated until the stone fails to reattach which indicates that the poison is gone. People throughout the region swore to its effectiveness and, in a period when rabies and snakebites more often than not lead to death, mad stones and their owners were much in demand.

In 1922, Otis Carter's son Artis was bitten by a rabid dog while playing at the home of Buford Redding. Otis had heard about owned by Mr. Arch Aydellot of Havana so he travelled the twenty-five miles over the mountain to pick it up. Mr. Aydellot had three of the stones which had been handed down to him from his great great grandfather. When used, the stone immediately attached to his son. After cleaning, he attempted to attach it a second time but it failed to attach which showed the poison was removed. The young man survived without further difficulty.

On another occasion, a man from Harkey Valley had been bitten by a rabid dog thirteen days previously. Dr. Heffington brought the man to Mr. Aydellot who applied the stone to the infected area. The first stone clung to the wound for sixteen hours, was cleaned and then clung to him for twelve hours during the second use. On the third attempt, the stone indicated the poison was gone and the man survived.

Seventh-sons and children born after their father's death are also subject of many beliefs and myths. Many believe children born of either of these two groups have specials insight and mythical abilities. Jim Millard's mother was pregnant with him when her husband died. Jim, raised near Dutch Creek, was known for having the "healing touch." Throughout the region, when a child was born, it was brought to Jim and he would blow into the child's mouth. None of the children would ever develop thrush. Danny, my youngest uncle, was also born after his father's death. People believed he could cure warts and skin illness simply by the power of touch. Seventh sons' supposedly have the ability to look at a person and read their minds, have healing power, and special blessings because the number seven is sacred and mentioned throughout the Bible.

Prickly Ash Tree

Many other such home remedies and cures were used by the hill people-often with amazing success. One of the more common is the use of the prickly-ash tree which is found in the mountains of Arkansas. The tree is usually small in size, has alternating leaf structure, and covered with spikes or needles. Probably adopted for use after seeing natives use the tree, it is used to treat skin disease, rheumatism, typhoid, and blood impurities. The most common use is to alleviate tooth aches by chewing bark extracted from the tree. As many locals can attest, it has a nearly instantaneous numbing effect and lessens pain.

My grandmother Nettie often resorted to local herbs and medicine. Jerry, the uncle three years older than me, often lead Danny and I into mischief. At the ripe age of seven, he introduced me to cigarettes. Having found an entire pack of the Salem brand, he divided them between the three of us with the admonition that, not only did we have to smoke our share, we had to inhale

the smoke and exhale it through our nose. I gagged and sniffed, burned and spit and finally was able to burn up a couple of the ones he provided.

That night, while staying at my grandmothers with the two uncles, I became violently ill with an extreme stomach ache. With Jerry present, I couldn't tell my grandmother what had happened without becoming Jerry's punching bag the next morning. Fumbling around by the light of the lamp, grandma constructed me a potent concoction of kerosine (coal oil) and sugar. Holding my nose, she poured a spoonful of the gritty mixture down my throat. Not only did it help my stomach ache, it completely cured me of any desire to ever smoke again. I am not sure it was from lessening any foolish desire I might have had as it was the fear that any fire constructed near my mouth might cause instantaneous internal explosion from the fuel provided in my medication.

Isolation and reliance on living off the land also contributed to the unique cuisine found only among the hill people. Called "country cooking," the diet relies heavily on potato, corn bread, brown beans, and pork. Generally, everything is fried and dosed heavily with lard, salt, and/or butter. Until after the Civil War, many homes had unattached kitchens where cooking was conducted. Often completed over open fireplaces, food was cooked in iron skillets, Dutch ovens, and other utensils that could be used over the open flame.

The cast iron stove was much safer and easier to use. They became readily available to most families in the years after the Civil War and were used extensively in most homes in the shadow of the mountains. The one above is typical and consisted of a fire box, an enclosed oven and two to six burners covered by removable iron plates. Typical of most families in the area with large families, my grandmother would arise early in the morning and prepare a huge breakfast. This involved frying a dozen or so eggs consisting of everything from sunny-side up to solid yolk. Pork was the most readily available meat and breakfast consisted of salt-cured ham, bacon, hog jowl, or sausage.

In the period after the Civil War, cornmeal was the most readily available substance from which to make bread. It was served as the typical cornbread, fired over the stove as fritters, and dusted over every vegetable possible as a coating. No squash, onion, or okra is ever complete without being doused with cornmeal and fried.

A huge pan of biscuits was constructed each morning from scratch. The baking pan measured about eighteen inches long and about half as wide. Biscuits were several inches thick and, during breakfast, were slathered with butter, molasses, or jelly. When ingredients were available, three types of gravies were constructed. Red eye gravy was made from pork drippings (grease), salt, and coffee. The coffee dissolved and sat in the middle of the puddle of grease, lending the name "red-eye." Regular milk gravy was a part of virtually every meal and still is a tradition in the south. My favorite, and one virtually unheard of outside the Scotch-Irish, is chocolate gravy which is a type of pudding served hot and with quantities of butter over biscuits. Remains of breakfast were stuck between divided biscuit halves and placed in lard can buckets which were used for lunch. Mid-morning snack for women would often consist of the aforementioned biscuits, covered with sugar, and doused with coffee.

Supper usually consisted of garden or canned vegetables, more fried pork, corn bread, beans, and fried potato. Even if we had chicken, wild game, or beef steak, it was still fried. Until food chains from up North invaded, most Scotch-Irish didn't know you could bake, baste, broil, or grill any type of meat and the only vegetarian known to exist were those who couldn't hunt or were too poor to buy meat.  Yankee's have their meals all mixed up. The meal served at lunch is dinner, the evening meal, as anyone with half-a-brain knows, is supper. This confusion on the part of people north of the Mason-Dixon line has led to a host of problems throughout my life. After breakfast, I never knew what meal they were referring to, but being perpetually hungry, I always showed up whenever told food was prepared. It took me two years of college to discover that evening classes meant those after six P.M. Evening to the Scotch means any time after the noon meal.

Scotch-Irish are very "clan" oriented and family and friends are expected to visit. At the turn of the century, people commonly visited each other in the evening hours, shared meals, or just sit on the porch and talked. A practice derived from the "Old Country", the Scotch-Irish tended to congregate around the home of the oldest member of the family. This was especially true on Sundays and, unless fighting with a family member, you were expected to show up. The preferred menu usually included fried chicken and accompanying potato, gravy, biscuits, dessert, and tea so sweet a spoon wouldn't sink in it.

Some of our more unique fare included a mixture of tomato and bread called slum gulley, poke salad and eggs, a gelatinous dessert called jam cake, pineapple pudding, fried squirrel head, squirrel dumplings, tomato gravy, and myriad other delicacies that probably could not be sold in a public restaurant. Many of these foods are derivatives of food prepared for generations in the old country. Others are those derived from "making do" with whatever ingredients were available to the hill people. If you had a large family and a quart jar of canned tomato and a quart of boiled okra, you mixed the two, threw in salt and spices and instantly became a "chef" of distinction from the resulting concoction- a common hill dish called tomato okra soup. Served with corn bread, it would "stick to your ribs" and get your through a hard day of work.

Scotch-Irish had a particular order of precedence at meal time. Babies were sometimes fed early as the women prepared the meal. Next, all the men were seated and fed, then came the children, and the women ate last. This was an unquestioned practice that we accepted as universal until straightened out by our more sophisticated wives.

Scotch-Irish tends to be conservative in politics and religion. Historically, the Scotch-Irish has been fiercely independent and has held little faith in government and its promises. When they arrived in America in the early 1700's, very little land was available along the seacoast. As a result, they journeyed to the frontier along the Appalachians and struggled to survive. As the leading edge of the Western movement, they fought the Indian wars and pushed into the interior of the United States. Daniel Boone, Rogers Clark, and other explorers and mountain men were of Scotch extraction. They often felt excluded from the eastern establishment and the decisions made in Washington. Some of the earliest settlers cleared the land, fought the Indian, and established farms only to lose their property to land speculators and others who had established legal paperwork. Andrew Jackson and men of his type were viewed as heroes and most mountain people have several in their lineage named Andrew Jackson, Daniel Boone, or even Lafayette. Heroes were viewed as men who knew what they wanted in life and willing to grasp it even if it meant a fight.

Many in Arkansas actually received ownership of property as a result of fighting alongside Jackson at New Orleans during the Battle of New Orleans. When they arrived in Arkansas to establish their claims, little government existed so these men were used to depending on their own wiles and wishes. The Scotch-Irish could be described as men with a chip on their shoulder- often deservedly so from their treatment by establishments in the Old Country (Northern Ireland, England, and even the Netherlands). When more established government arrived, it was often looked upon with distrust.

The Scotch-Irish were religious dissidents. They were part of the Protestant Revolution that had taken place in Europe in the two centuries prior to their arrival in America. Followers of John Calvin, they were known as Presbyterians, Puritans, and Huguenots. Some, influenced by John Wesley, had established the Methodist church in Scotland. Placed in Northern Ireland as a counter-force to the Catholic population, they had multiplied rapidly into a riotous group that eventually became Northern Ireland.

As early as 1819, Henry Schoolcraft mentions encountering an itinerant minster near the White

Union School House and Church, Paris

River that was preaching to a group of hunters. By early 1820, Methodist, Baptist, and Cumberland Presbyterians record sending preachers to minister to the growing numbers of settlers in the state.

One of the largest early denominations in Arkansas was he Cumberland Presbyterian Church. Established in 1810 in Kentucky, its

ministers could honor the divine "call" to the ministry without going through the formal

educational process of the Presbyterians. The Cumberland Presbyterians established

congregations across the state and had large numbers adherents in the Cane Hill community near

Fayetteville. Many of the early Baptists and Methodists were

also men of faith who answered the "call" with much more

zeal than education, a situation that seemed to work just fine

with the scattered rural congregations of Arkansas.

Most of these ministers arrived to find there were no

established congregations, no church buildings, and little

monetary support for their work. Pay was either non-existent

or extremely low and most of the ministers had to farm or

hire out their labor in order to survive. Arkansas's population

Rev. Hansel Trusty

was small and scattered. As a result, it was often necessary of a minister to be a "circuit"

minister. As such, he would minister to several congregations by setting up a monthly schedule of services scattered between several communities. In areas where no church existed, the minister would arrange a "camp meeting" revival." These were usually arranged during the summer time after the crops were planted and prior to harvest. People from miles around would gather near good springs and water sources, set up a brush covered arbor, and have nightly meetings that would sometimes go on for weeks.

When possible, rustic churches constructed of logs were built. These were often shared as school houses during the week and churches on Sundays. In small communities, circuit ministers took turns holding services for their congregations. Because these churches were *united* into one building, the schools were often referred to as Union schools. Union school house, built in 1895 near Paris, functioned as one such building and still stands today. It was used by the Cumberland Presbyterian church, community groups, and as a school.

Pastoral salaries were low. Methodist preachers in 1833 were paid $34 per year if they were single, double that if they were married. More than twenty years later, an article in *The Christian Repository* stated that Baptist preachers were averaging less than $200 a year, and some were responsible for three or four churches. Preachers of all denominations farmed, taught school, or owned businesses to make ends meet. They were often paid "in kind" with garden vegetables, eggs, or hand-me-down clothes for their children. Few congregations provided housing for the preacher. Reverend Bingaman, one of the early circuit riding Cumberland Presbyterian ministers, would ride from Midway to the Mount Salem church for service and might receive a quarter, a couple dimes, and lunch for his salary.

Paris First Methodist

Paris and Booneville established Methodist Churches as soon as they became established towns.

Smaller churches and circuits existed at New Blaine, Mount Salem, Shoal Creek, Prairie View, Magazine, and other small communities.

Baptist Churches existed in many of the same communities as did the Church of Christ. Mountain people are and were attracted to churches featuring hard preaching, loud music, and enthusiastic worship. Revivals offered the clannish groups a chance to meet, visit, and to hold communal dinners on the ground. In the summer after crops were "laid by," revivals lasting for

Subiaco Abbey and Academy

weeks would be conducted. Often held in brush arbors or old schoolhouses, the churches featured raised stages, hard plank rail benches, and music from a variety of instruments.

Large numbers of German Catholic were lured into the area immediately after the Civil War. Railroads were given huge tracts of land lying along their path of construction. Railroad magnates realized that they had to have people and products to deliver to make money and the best way to do this was to settle the land along the railroad tracks. The Little Rock and Fort Smith railroad company negotiated with a Benedictine Abbot from Indiana to get them to establish a monastery and church near Subiaco. In return, the order was given 640 acres of land for the establishment of a monastery for men. An additional 100 acres of land was provided to establish a monastery for women. The original abbey was established south of present day Subiaco on March 15, 1878 and a women's monastery was established near New Blaine. The hard-working monks soon established a working farm, rock quarry from which they cut stone for a church, and other commercial endeavors.

German settlers soon followed and built communities and churches in Morrison Bluff, Scranton, Paris, and at Shoal Creek.

After a fire and other problems, the Benedictine monks built the beautiful edifice that graces the hill just north of highway 22. Attached to the Abbey is one of the foremost Catholic Academies for boys in the U.S. The site has been visited over the years by many famous individuals, none more famous than sitting President Bill Clinton, who visited the Abbey to celebrate the wedding of a close friend.

Scotch-Irish worked side by side with the new German-Catholic neighbors for years with each group maintaining their identity. Because of religious differences, there was little intermarriage between the groups. This was a major problem for many area youth because the girls of German descent were so attractive and most of the girls in the local community were relatives. Not understanding this norm, David Rhinehart and I decided to visit one of the local Catholic families that happened to have several young ladies of about our age. We were made welcome by the girls and their perplexed mother and sat on the porch swigging tea until the father arrived home. He had been hard at work in the rock quarries all day and was covered with dust and sweat. A huge man, he strolled briskly up to the porch like a dog-tired man happy to be home, that is until he saw the two teen male visitors. His face turned red, veins stood out on his forehead, as he glared from underneath bushy red eyebrows. "You boys from over at Midway," he asked in deeply accented English. About that time, I was remembering the admonishment given to me at home to stay away from the Catholic girls. We both scrambled to our feet; "Yes, Sir," we replied. Having fifteen year old voices to start with and now alarmed as well, we probably sounded like two prime candidates for the soprano section of the Mormon Choir. "I know your daddies boy, and there good men but they ain't a one of my girls going with anyone but a good Catholic boy. Now, you boys just finish up that tea and just head on home." The girls, friendly and vociferous just moments before now sat in silence with their heads down. He pushed past us and opened the screen, his posture and stiff stride indicating his unhappiness at finding us in the neighborhood. David and I received instantaneous inspiration, first to leave the place as soon as possible and second, to visit Catholic girls only when they were at 4-H meetings or at Scranton ballgames. David went on to marry into the Catholic Schneider family of Paris.

The irate father made a greater impression on me; I stayed over in our valley and married the first girl that moved into the neighborhood I wasn't related to.

The other major irritation with

Cowie Winery, Museum near Paris

116

Catholic groups was their diet. We cared little if their food was heavily influenced with pork, blood sausage, and other German delicacies but we did care that Catholics could eat no meat on Fridays. Protestant, Catholic, or atheist, we all invariably received the same school lunch on Fridays. School cooks are great but you can only do so much with fish sticks. Someone, probably Mrs. Hudson the school dietician, decided that those fish sticks go well with green mashed potato salad, green beans, and a peach half. If the Pope every decreed that we had to extend that lunch through lent, half of the school populations would have died of starvation. One other large difference between Catholic and the Puritanical Scotch-Irish was the consumption of alcohol. Although condoned in the Catholic areas, the only alcohol found in the mountain area was distilled corn whiskey.

With a large Catholic population, North Logan County voted semi-wet which meant that wine and beer could be bought and sold on premise. Taverns selling liquor could be found in the coal mining towns of Paris and Scranton and in the Catholic community of Subiaco. Wine was produced by many of the Catholic

Kennedy Tavern, Subiaco

families in the county and a wine cellar and museum owned by the Cowie family is located in Carbon City.

One of the busiest businesses was Steed Kennedy's tavern at Subiaco. While working at Warehouse Market in Paris, I was asked by the butcher to drop off a box of dog bones for Mr.

117

Kennedy. Not wanting to walk through the tavern, I circled the store to get to the Kennedy home. Heavily laden with the large box of bones, I rounded the corner of the tavern and was

 confronted by the meanest guard animal known to man. The animals head dipped parallel to the ground as it began to hiss and stalk me. The red beady eyes glowed with malicious intent as it advanced slowly in my direction. Suddenly, with a ferocious squawk, the animal charged directly at me. With gapping beak and flapping wings, the animal was on me before I could move. Realizing the impossibility of winning the confrontation, I threw down the box and took to my heels in flight. The animals hot breath flowed over my back as it firmly assaulted my posterior with its beak and wings. Rounding the corner of the store in full flight and screaming for help, I meet Stead clothed in apron and armed with his broom. Applying the broom briskly to the huge gander, Stead rescued me from the wild goose. Escaping into the safe confines of my car, I realized that every patron of his business was standing outside the store and had watched the debacle. Totally chagrined and with loss of any false pride I might have had, I drove off, little realizing that the goose guard was part of the daily entertainment at the tavern.

Running a still is supposedly a tradition in the hills. Many rumors circulated about various neighbors who disappeared into the hills on a regular basis to manufacture the high alcohol content liquid. Stills were known to exist at near Shoal Bay, near Midway, and at various sites on Huckleberry, Rich, and Magazine Mountain. Whiskey was an efficient and cheap way to turn excess corn into a product that was easily marketable and profitable. A few bushels of corn, yeast, sugar, and water would yield several gallons of a product that could be easily transported to markets in Little Rock, Memphis, or New Orleans. This was especially true during the days of prohibition.

Although frowned upon severely by the local Protestant churches, more than a few gallons were consumed locally, often with serious consequences. Law officials ranging from James Garner, the first Logan County sheriff, to Pete Carter and even to the current sheriff often repeat their experiences in tracing down offenders. During the height of the depression, several stills were built in Shoal Creek hollow. Several of the young men, not attuned to the hazards associated with imbibing more than a few ounces of the 160 proof brew, were known to get rip-roaring drunk. One of the young men, explaining his

actions to his family in the days following the incident, explained. "It was in a heck of fight. I knocked the snot out of him. Blood was flowing from his nose and he was lying on the ground begging me to stop. I beat him up good. I didn't know till the next morning it was ___(his brother)."

On another occasion, one local Mutt and Jeff pair decided, after a few too many drinks, to invite themselves to a party held by the Wise and Lewis's family. Both families were descendants of former slaves and owned extensive property along Shoal Creek, near present day Hamilton horse camp. Stumbling down the path that followed the creek, the two drinkers happened upon the party. Several friends and relatives had journeyed to join the Wise party. They had thrown up a small dance platform and arranged for a band to play as they danced.

When Mutt and Jeff arrived, the party was in full swing. Huge tables laden with food sat in the shadows of the trees. Older people sat in groups, gossiping and exchanging small tales while kids rolled around playing in the sandy dust.

Older couples and singles were having a great time swinging each other around the dance floor and enjoying the sounds of the band.

The two young drunks decided, with probably more than a little racial bigotry, that they would join the merrymaking. Mr. Wise was well known and respected around the neighborhood. He had raised several children and grandchildren and generally got along with everyone. The two young men started out by helping themselves to the food, all the while being loud and obnoxious. Stumbling upon the dance floor, they began to hoot, holler and shuffle, proving without a doubt that they could not dance. Grabbing the young ladies, they began swinging them in faster and faster circles, laughing and falling down, only to get up and continue. Both men ignored the requests for them to leave.

Several of the Wise and Lewis family were strong strapping fellows, heavily muscled from working in the fields and lumber yards. Finally, deciding they had suffered enough from the drunks, one of the young men reached down, grabbed the ankles of Jeff. Jeff, all five foot four or so of him, was jerked rudely upside down and held by his ankles. The band played on while the tall Wise offspring danced with the upside down Jeff. The short man's head banged up and down off the platform as the waltzed across the stage, the debut of the pogo duo. At the same time, the larger Mutt was getting himself off the ground beneath the platform from which he had fallen. Looking like Floyd from the Andy Griffith show, his rheumy red eyes beheld the unusual sight before him. Known to be one of the toughest and best fighters in the area, the liquor and courage both failed him in the same instant. Down the road he flew, followed seconds later by his sore-headed buddy.

While working at Warehouse Market grocery, one of our regular customers would send his wife in to purchase groceries. All the while, he sat in his old red flatbed truck imbibing and sharing his product with his large basset hound. The hound would take a large sip out of the tin dipper, roll his mournful red eyes at you, and then plop his head back down on the truck seat. The grizzled old-timer would laugh, take a sip from the same container, and stay happy in his soul while waiting on his spouse. After declining his offer to share a nip of the clear liquid, he extolled the virtues of its use, explained that he bought it for sixteen dollars a gallon, and then shared the secret of where he purchased his supply. To my surprise, a short walk from my home in Midway would have placed me at the source of the still.

It was perhaps from this still that local bootleggers purchased a trunk load of hooch to transport to Oklahoma. Stopped by State police near the hilltop café on Sand Ridge, they waited until the trooper walked up beside their car and then sped rapidly away. Not to be deprived of his arrest, the young trooper drew his weapon and fired three quick shots at the escaping vehicle. The car quickly came to a halt and the trooper again approached the vehicle noting the huge amount of liquid pouring from beneath the trunk. Investigating, what began as a simple speeding ticket turned into a full investigation involving gallons of illegal Arkansas moonshine.

Arkansas has always had conflicting views on alcohol- those became even more convoluted after the demise of prohibition. At that time, each county was given the right to determine alcohol

 sales. Many of the mountain people voted completely dry. This included Johnson, Scott, and Yell Counties. Other counties were more divided on the issue and allowed complete sale of alcohol. Franklin,

Logan, and Sebastian Country were so divided on the issue that the counties ended up with some townships wet, some dry, and some, like those in North Logan County, that were semi-wet and allowed beer, wine, and low proof alcohol.

Similar to attitudes about alcohol, most of the Scotch-Irish was adamantly opposed to the introduction of illegal drugs into the community. By the 1970's, drug culture had drifted into the hills. While few people used heroin, cocaine, or the harder drugs; marijuana use and growth were becoming widespread. The same hollows, caves, and secretive hideouts used by Civil War soldiers were now being used as hide-outs and hidden gardens by those evading the law. Arkansas climate seemingly was very conducive to its growth and Logan County Sheriffs Dub Hamilton and Jim King and Ed Wolf of the State Police found themselves constantly involved in tracking down perpetrators. While most of the residents were adamantly opposed to any drug use, they are so independent minded and fearful of government control that they failed to offer assistance to those enforcing the law. The prevailing attitude is to kind of shrug your shoulders and state, "Well, I don't use that stuff and don't want my family involved but as long as they stay on their place, I'm not sticking my nose in their business." Typical of mountain folks, this attitude prevails to modern times and has contributed to the continuing problems found with the manufacturing and use of meth and other drugs that are killing the future of children and young adults in the region.

During the 1980's, Wiley and Fanny Rhineheart lived just south of Midway on the Sorghum Hollow road. Wiley was an old farmer, lumberjack, and long-time resident of the area. Jack Sanders, one of many of my uncles, bought five acres of land and moved a house trailer in just across the street. Jack, always a character and looking for a way to make a fast dollar, decided to grow marijuana on his property. Jack was an indifferent farmer when growing up on the family farm in Okemah, Oklahoma but had much more incentive to produce a bumper crop in Arkansas.

All of the family was amazed by his sudden interest in developing a garden. He plowed up the

land, fertilized it heavily and even developed an irrigation system.

To avoid getting caught, he placed his "special" crop in the center of his garden and concealed it

by growing tall stands of corn around the periphery of

the plot. Each time we passed his home on our way

to the half-bushel swimming hole, he could be seen

out tending his crop. The corn grew huge, green and

bushy with big ears sprouting at right angles to the

stalk. We were absolutely amazed by his ability.

Tomato Garden

Jack was always an outgoing, fun type of guy so he got

to visiting Wiley on a regular basis. They would sit out on the big front porch, rocking in their

chairs, and talk about the world's problems. Jack would ask about best methods to use in

farming and Wiley would provide all the "low down" that he had accumulated over the years.

Wiley was also quite impressed by Jack's ability to grow a good looking plant but was really

worried about his crop production rate. While talking with Man Miller at the Midway store, Jeff

Miller heard Wiley exclaim, " you know, that Jack is a good neighbor. I've got so I really like

sitting around visiting with him over to the house but I worry about the boy. He grew some good

corn and some vegetables. He's got the best looking tomato plants in the center of that garden I

have ever seen. Them things are five foot or more tall but, you, know, he ain't got a tomato one

off them plants. I know he's disgusted. Me an Fanny got so worried about him, we gave him a

peck of tomatoes from our own garden." Jeff, a little more knowledgeable about such things

was still laughing about it twenty years later.

Jack eventually was caught by Dub Hamilton, spent all of one night in jail before making bail, and got out of the business. Jack eventually made things right, joined the Baptist Church, and died at an early age. In his later years, he explained how he escaped his dilemma by paying twenty-thousand dollars under the table to the judge and lawyer to escape punishment.

Talk to the people of the mountain and you will find them little changed. The basic beliefs and concepts held by forefathers are still very evident within the region. Overwhelmingly, scratch the surface of their believes or listen to explanations of how they vote, you will find the people hard-working, family oriented, religious, conservative, and loyal. They are also suspicious of outsiders, distrusting of too much government control, clannish, and quite sure their way of life is superior. Get one or more of them mad, you have a fight on your hands but, treated as fairly and as an equal, you have one of the best workers, neighbors, and friends in the world. Such are the ridge runners and valley people!!

Into the 20th Century

The New South faced many problems as it emerged from the period of Reconstruction. Prior to the Civil War, Arkansas was viewed as a very progressive state that abounded in opportunities. People were rapidly pouring into the state. The population stood at 210,000 in 1850; by 1860 the population had more than doubled to 435,000. Much of the state was devastated by the war. People fled the state in every direction and many never returned. Former slaves headed North, seeking new opportunities and greater freedom. People that had supported the Southern cause lost their political and civil rights as well as much of their property. Prior to the war, much of their wealth had been tied up in purchasing slaves at great expense. A healthy slave in their prime was valued at more than $1,200 dollars. The large plantations of the delta, with dozens of slaves, lost tremendous amounts of money. Combined with the devastation of buildings and grounds due to war, owners had no collateral to use to obtain loans. Dozens were thrown into bankruptcy or simply left the land. Carpetbaggers and scoundrels flooded into the region, looking for quick ways to improve their lot in life. Many became involved in politics, others bought up land and began farming.

The demand for cotton and the scarcity of labor created the demand for a new system of labor. Land owners could hire labor to work the farms at the going rate of $13 per month for men and $9 per month for women. With cash not readily available, owners and laborers devised the system of tenant farming. The tenant farmer was given a parcel of land, generally forty acres, and implements to raise cotton. In return, he was paid from twenty-five to fifty percent of the profit from the crop. Since cotton prices varied according to supply, during many years there was little profit to share.

In the mountains and valleys of the River Valley, life did not revolve as much around the production of cotton. Many of the farmers raised other crops and livestock and raised what little cotton they could as a money crop. Virtually every floodplain and level spot in the region has been used for farming- much of it for cotton.

At one time, Robert Parson's farmed the second bench of Rich Mountain. The land is difficult to access with steep slopes and a narrow, rocky bench but it would grow cotton in good years. Others grew cotton on benches on both sides of Magazine Mountain and extensive crops were raised along the Arkansas and Petit Jean Rivers.

Even though freed, former slaves found life difficult. Released without means of support, without education, and without a background that prepared them for life, many found themselves back in virtual servitude as tenant farmers or sharecroppers. Remarkable was the man who could overcome these handicaps and become a valued member of the community in which they lived. Willis Wise is one of those exceptional individuals that overcome adversity and carved out a life for himself in the new South.

Willis was born a slave in Boston, Texas on January 8, 1849. Not much is known about his early life or the reason for him migrating to Logan County, Arkansas after the war. Many slaves fled to Arkansas from Louisiana, Texas, and Mississippi during the war and joined Union forces. For whatever reason, Willis found his way into the mountains. In 1870, he married Mary Christopher, a former slave from Clarksville, Arkansas and they bought land and built a log cabin on Shoal Creek near where Hamilton's horse camp now stands.

Willis and Mary Wise in the center; Fannie Mae Wise in the middle of the front row, Mint Wise in the hat to the far right, Ella (Wise) Thompson is next to her. Beginning in the second row from the left is Clara (Wise) Lewis holding a baby and Sellars Newton is next to her. From the top right is Frank Thompson holding a baby, and center top is Hardy Wise. (Dortha Terwey)

Willis was a farmer and found the land along the creek rich in soil but also covered with rock brought down by the creek and with lowland hardwood. Clearing the land would have been a difficult task but one that Willis was obviously successful in accomplishing. He was a skilled basket maker and weaved both large and small baskets from the cane along the creek. He would take his old mule laden with baskets and pedal them throughout the region. Large baskets were used to harvest cotton so there was a good market for his products. Willis was successful enough at his various enterprises that his family was able to start a church and a school and organize a small black community in a predominantly white township. Willis would arrange to have visiting ministers from Memphis, Oklahoma, and other black communities to visit and hold

127

revivals at his church which he called the Home Mission Baptist Church. He loved to play the fiddle and was an accomplished musician.

Around 1890, his wife started working with Dr. B.M. Miller. He taught her many of the herbs and medicines and how to deliver babies. For more than forty years after he left the community, "Aunt Mary" continued tending the sick and delivering babies. Sometimes she would remain at their homes for days and weeks tending to the needs of both white and black patients.

Because the Wise family lived on the south side of Shoal Creek, it was often difficult to travel to St. Louis Valley or north toward the town of Shoal Creek. During the spring or during rainy seasons, the small stream would become a raging torrent. It often overflowed its banks, carrying huge trees and tumbling rocks as big as a small houses. The low water fords that they normally crossed at St. Louis Valley road or on what is now Methodist Camp road were impassable. Her grandson Sellars Newton drove her around with a fast horse and buggy- way too fast for her taste. He later traded for a T-Model car but it was undependable and, when the creek rose, he wasn't able to get it across. During bad weather he would beg her to stay home only to be told, "Son, it's my duty." She was never known to refuse to assist anyone.

Willis and Mary had ten children: James, Oliver, Ella, Beeda, Sophia, Will, Hardie, Charles, Minta, and Clara. They would hire teachers to come in and teach three month terms to educate their children.

Clara Wise (Lewis) was able to get the minimum eighth grade education required at that time to become a teacher. She taught several generation of students at Shoal Creek and later, at Gray Rock schools. Because of the scarcity of schools, the preponderance of whites, and the degree that she was respected in the community, she is believed to have taught the first integrated classes in Arkansas.

Willis passed away on January 16, 1933 and Mary lived to the age of 107. When she died, she requested the funeral be conducted by her good friend and white Midway Assembly of God minister, Reverend P.W. Wright to conduct the funeral. Both they and other family members are buried in Mays cemetery at the present day Shoal Creek Methodist Youth Camp.

During the 1940's, many of the community left in search of work or better opportunities. Clark and Clara (Wise) moved to Gray Rock where she continued working as a teacher. At the time of Mary Wise death, she had acquired 72 grandchildren, 64 great grandchildren, and 6 great-great-grandchildren. Many of the descendants of this family still live in the area.

As people review life from a century ago, they often talk about the difficulty families faced. People living a hundred years from now will probably feel the same way about our life today. It is true that people had to work hard and that farming was very labor intensive during the growing seasons. The people living through the period knew good times, had winter days with little to do, visited neighbors in the evenings, attended church functions, and probably generally enjoyed life. Food, entertainment, travel, communication, education, and much of what we think of necessities today were much simpler but were balanced by sense of community, family, and faith of their time period.

Most homes in the area were simple dogtrot homes made of logs or rough lumber. As one obtained more property and wealth, larger frame homes were constructed and additional outbuildings were added. Joseph Horn family owned an extensive valley between Wright Hill and Pine Ridge. His children first constructed a log cabin and then began to construct a frame home just across the road. The new home sat high off the ground, supported by rock pilings that supported the floors. A large porch was constructed across the front; a place to sleep during the hot summer nights and a place to visit neighbors that happened by. Originally most homes had wood shakes for the roof. Nearly every small town had a shake mill that cut these roofing materials from the abundant trees in the area. As the family obtained more wealth, they bought sheet metal to overlay the shakes, a definite advantage because the shakes had a tendency to swell and shrink with the weather resulting in numerous leaks. Heating was accomplished with fireplaces, often placed on both ends of the main house.

Horn Farm, Pine Ridge Arkansas

Since many of the homes were made from untreated lumber, the boards would often warp resulting in large cracks in the floors. People often remarked that they could count chickens under the house by looking through the cracks. Inside walls and ceilings were covered by another layer of rough wood. Wind and cold could always find its way through the walls. To prevent this, many families covered the walls with old newspaper as a means of insulation. Nice wallpaper or plaster was expensive so many families would purchase large rolls of colored paper, pink appeared to be a favorite color or was cheapest, and these were unrolled over the newspapers and held down by large brass tacks. These still did little to provide insulation and fireplaces often heated areas only directly in front of them. Later, pot-bellied coal or wood burning iron stoves connected to metal stove pipes with dampers provided better heating. Many cold evenings were spent around metal stoves that glowed cherry red from the heat within. The coal-oil lamp would cast shadows around the room and off the walls as family and friends sat around the stove and shared stories of life.

Outhouses provided the restroom of the period. Constructed of left over lumber, they were simply seats over open-drop holes. Smelly, hot in the summer and cold in the winter, they are one thing most people of today would enjoy being without.

Outhouses enjoyed a special place in the pranks of the day. Into the 1960's, many homes were serviced by these outdoor facilities. Young pranksters would continually push them over, nail the doors shut and, on more than one occasion, bodily place them in unlikely places. Woodard Mosely arrived at his store in Midway on many occasions to find the restroom balanced on the apex of his stores roof. He was usually pretty calm about it but his wife Flossy would probably have shot one of the culprits if she could locate them.

Everett Mullins lived on Midway hill just east of highway 109. An avowed and permanent bachelor, his home served as a visiting place for many of the unmarried men in the community. Never a driver, he would always hitch rides with whomever was traveling to Paris on the weekend or, in his later years, travel anywhere with someone wanting a companion to talk with. Well liked, he was also the target of many pranks carried out around the area.

Sitting at the Midway store during a warm fall evening, several of the young men of the community decided to sneak up the hill to Everett's home and push his bathroom over. They could see light glowing from his windows as they crept up the hill behind his outhouse. Silently, they crept behind the building. All three boys leaned into the building, pushing with all of their strength. As the building began to tip forward with their efforts, they were shocked to hear Everett screeching inside, "Boys, boys, I'm in here. Put my toilet down." Panicked, they continued with their efforts. The toilet tottered and then fell forward with a crash. Jerry Varnell, located in the center of the boys pushing the toilet, lost balance from his efforts and tumbled into the abyss. Pandemonium reigned! Scraping and rolling sounds were heard from within the toilet as it occupant tumbled about. Everett was now pleading, "Guys, please sit the toilet up. I can't get out of here." The latter was a true statement since the bathroom door was now on the bottom of the building. Jerry was floundering knee deep in the toilet hole, struggling to extract himself. Seeing his dilemma, Sammy Bowman grasped Jerry by the arm and yanked him from the pit. All three boys headed down the hill in a blind flight with Everett's pleas ringing in their ears. Jerry was retching, overcome by near-death experience. "We can't leave that old man trapped in the toilet, whispered Sammy, a worried expression on his long, freckled face. He ain't got a family. He might lay in there for days before somebody gets him out." "Fellows, we got to help him, returned Herbert, but I can't get caught. Dad will take the skin off me if he finds out." Devising a plan, the three crept back up the hill. Everett could still be heard moaning and groaning within the ramshackle outhouse. Reaching down and grasping the door, Jerry held it closed while Herbert and Sammy grasped the corners and heaved upward. Filled with adrenaline, they hoisted the building skyward, again shuffling the old man topsy-turvy in the outhouse. Back down the hill they ran as fast as feet could carry them, the outhouse still tottering back and forth before settling into place.

The Horn place, like many of the period, was built near a spring. Springs are found along the bottom of ridges and hill and occur when water falling on the surface hits an impermeable layer of rock and flows laterally to the surface. The water from most of the springs is good to drink and exits the earth in the mid-50 degrees, about the average temperature of Arkansas. Many families cleaned around the exit point of their spring and built a spring house over it. The spring house served as the refrigerator. The cooler temperatures allowed fresh milk, meats, and vegetables to be stored. Cream was allowed to "clabber" and then was churned into butter with the remains drank as buttermilk. Many of the farmers made money by selling excess butter and eggs to those living in towns.

Root vegetables such as turnips and potatoes were stored in cellars along with canned vegetables.

Canning in class "mason" jars had become a popular way of preserving food in post-Civil War years and involved placing food in jars and preserving under high temperatures and pressure. Mason jars by the hundreds were filled with blackberries, vegetables, peaches, and even canned meats. These canned goods could be preserved for periods of up to five years and the goods within them helped families survive during winters and droughts.

Most families raised poultry, a few cattle, and pigs to supplement what wild game they could obtain. The last buffalo in the state were killed in Saline County in 1867 and most of the larger game such as bear, buffalo, and even deer were not in plentiful supply by the turn of the century. As a result, families became more and more dependent on pork. Pigs were a staple of life and were raised throughout the region.

Many of the first settlers marked the pig's ears and allowed them to run wild, harvesting them when winter arrived. Latter, pens were built and pigs were fed leftovers mixed with corn chops and bran called shorts.

Lindal Parsons raised several on the family farm- enough to feed most of the family. He kept a large five-gallon bucket in which he placed the family slops which consisted of left- over food,  potato peels, water, and rotten vegetables. When feeding time came, he would throw in shorts and corn and mix it before feeding the animals. Chuck Parsons, his nephew, was known for his many pranks. Always looking for excitement, he usually created a passel of it when he was around. Just a few weeks prior to the pig incident, he and Jack Turner had attempted to start the pot-bellied stove in Lindal's shop. Searching high and low, they failed to find a match anywhere. Jack was ready to give up when Chuck devised the fail proof plan of placing carbide on the wood within the stove. Mixing water on the carbide produces acetylene gas that was used in miner's lights. Placing several ounces of carbide onto the wood, Chuck quickly wet it down with water and inserted the striker from Lindal's welder into the copious amounts of acetylene that he produced. Instantly there was an explosion of preponderate dimensions. Fire shot from the front and top of the stove, smoke bellowed, and the stovepipe began a rapid ascent through the roof, and a tremendous roar filled the place. Part of Chuck's eyebrows and hair disappeared in the blast. Both boys stumbled around in shock at the devastation. The potbellied stove was in three pieces, the stovepipe was still traveling upward, and small fires burned fiercely here and there. Doing what any red-blooded American boys would do, they ran like crazy, leaving the scene of destruction behind.

Now, just a couple of weeks removed, things had settled down way too much for the pair. Kids at the time would purchase pure cinnamon liquid from the drug store, insert toothpicks into the bottle, and then suck the toothpicks. Jalapeño peppers were mild in comparison. One of my uncles had spilled some in his pants pocket while trying to extract a stick in Coach Clay's class and, too frightened to ask to go to the restroom, found it took all the skin off the leg by next class period. Lindal's slop bucket proved too much of a temptation. Chuck poured the entire bottle into the bucket.

Shortly after, Lindell feed the hogs. Both boys hid nearby and watched the show. The pigs gulped down the food, oblivious to special ingredients. With about half of the food gone, the potion began its work. White, ropey string of saliva dribbled from the pig's mouth, tears streamed from their eyes, and globs of snot began to pour from their nostrils. Suddenly, one of the pigs began a mad dash around the pen. Around and around he flew, quickly followed by his comrades. Pink eyes rolled back until only the milky white of the eye interior showed as they tossed their heads, throwing spittle into the air as they groaned, snorted, and whistled. Faster and faster they traveled around the pen while Lindell looked on helplessly wondering what was attacking his future dinner. Exhausted, one of pigs thrust his head and gaping mall into the black, stinking muck of the pen. Their eyes rolled in appreciation of the cooling mixture. Finally, sighing with relief, they fell onto their sides with their mouths still inserted in the mud. For days, Lindell worried about the loss of appetite of his pork crop.

Harvesting the hogs was often a community project. Untold number of mornings, the neighbors would have gathered in front of the Horne barn to butcher the yearly crop.

Horn Barn

Cold, frosty weather was butchering weather. The sun would be coming up in the east as the men arrived for the day's work. Few associated with the task forget the smell, sounds, and labor required to convert the pig into bacon, ham, and pork chops. A huge fire heated the vat of water into which the pig would be inserted. Smaller fires were built under black kettles, a task reserved for women and children. After the pigs were killed, they were hoisted into the air and inserted in the boiling vats. Weighing several hundred pounds, often block and tackle or hoists were needed to handle the animal. Bristles were scrapped off by hand and the fat layers were removed. These were often thrown directly into the kettles where the heat quickly separated out the lard from the harder "cracklings." Sometimes the fat was mixed directly with ashes and lye, heated and turned into bars of lye soap. Since there was little or no refrigeration, the hams, shoulders, and side meat were cured by rubbing with salt. They could be placed in the smoke house and slowly cooked over hickory chips to create bacon and hams. Intestines were extracted and cleaned to stuff sausage. The loin, liver, brain, and some of the other organs were divided by the workers and consumed within the following few days. The ears, tail, and head were boiled in the kettles to extract a gelatinous mixture poured into loaf pans and mixed with spices. This mixture congealed into a loaf called souse meat and was considered a delicacy to be made into sandwiches. It was said that everything except the squeal was harvested.

Farmers just to the west of the Horne's harvested so many pigs that they had extra pork and lard to sale to people living in Paris. So much of their product was transported to Paris and sold that the entire region was known as "Greasy Valley."

Cotton was the money crop for the region. The best farming lands were those located along the Petit Jean and Arkansas Rivers but farms were found throughout the county. Cotton was grown along the streams flowing to the river and even on the benches of Magazine Mountain.

Typically, farm wages in the 1860's were around fifteen dollars per month. Little cash was available so many people simply tenant farmed and received twenty-five to fifty percent of the money received from the sale of the cotton. So much cotton was produced in the South that prices often collapsed leaving farmers with little or no income. Even in the best of years, many of the farmers in the River Valley could produce only about a half-bale of cotton per acre, not nearly enough to support themselves.

Steamboat John Howard, Loaded with bales of cotton in 1889 on Ouachita River

Most small towns contained cotton gins which processed the cotton into bales for shipment. Steamboats journeyed upriver to Roseville, Dardanelle, Spadra, and Morrison Bluff to pick up cotton to be transported to mills in New Orleans.

Many local farmers, not able to make enough cash on their own farms, hired themselves out to large farmers along the river or in the Delta. Others found a source of income cutting trees and selling wood products. Many local communities had sawmills that shaped and sold railroad ties, staves for barrels, and shakes used in roofing buildings. Other small mills cut rough lumber which was then sold to larger mills to be processed.

Coal from fields in Clarksville, Paris, Coal Hill, Scranton, and Greenwood was being sold as fuel by the late 1800 and early 1900's. Railroads required tremendous amounts of coal and the bituminous and low-grade anthracite from local mines fueled the development of the rail system across the Southwest. Many locals found what was, for the time, high paying jobs at the mines. The Red Rooster, the Monkey Run, Jewell, and the Sunshine were just a few of the colorful names associated with the mines. By 1900, the average salary was about ten cents an hour. For that amount, miners crawled into the damp, dark holes and risked life and limb from sunup to dark. Injury from falling rock, cave explosions, mechanical failure, and drowning were daily obstacles. Louis Biazo was typical of the early coalminers. His family was Italian immigrants and moved to the River Valley to obtain work. The young Louis, who could speak only Italian, was sent to Subiaco Academy to learn English and to obtain a rudimentary education. He soon returned home and began working in the mines with his father. He continued to do so until he was killed in a mine cave-in in 1944. His son Lindell followed him into the business, making three generations of coal miners.

May of 1929 was a very wet spring. Located near Vache Creek, the land above the mine was subject to frequent flooding. C.E. (Sam Carter) arrived early at the Greenwood 2 mine to check out the tunnel before the main crew arrived. Greenwood 2 was a huge mine. Connected to Fidelity, it ran about a mile east to west and a half-mile north to

Paris Coal Miner Monument

South. Every few hundred feet, the main tunnel branched into side channels called breasts. As Sam returned from the far end of the main shaft, he began to notice accumulations of water on the tunnel floor. Suddenly, with a roar, a wall of water tumbled toward Sam, filling the cavity from top to bottom. Terrified, Sam was swept up by the stream and carried back down the tunnel. Frantically, he grabbed for a handhold and caught the electric line suspended along the ceiling. Holding on with all his strength, he began to pull himself hand over hand back toward the mouth of the mine. Virtually exhausted, he finally pulled himself out of the water at breast 13. Stumbling though the darkness and praying for safety, he finally meets a crew of individuals sent down into the mine to rescue him. Years later, he described the event as the most horrifying day of his life. His son choose a safer occupation and served as pastor of the Missionary Baptist Church in Paris for more than forty years.

For most families in the River Valley, life was a constant struggle to make ends meet. Life was simple, work was hard, and life revolved around community, church, and family.

Life would change, new opportunities would present themselves, and the people of the River Valley would become more urban but that period awaited the advent of electricity, radio, television, the automobile and the conclusion of two great World Wars.

Barnets Store, Caulksville about 1900

A Question of Innocence

In the next few years, Fort Smith will complete and open the National Marshalls museum. The Arkansas River Valley is a natural location for this monument for law and order. Beginning immediately after the Civil War, Fort Smith housed the Federal Court responsible for law and order along the frontier, especially in the Indian Territory.

Judge Isaac Parker is best remembered at the "Hanging Judge" and is the product of legend as well as modern movies. More than seventy men were found guilty in his courts and were hanged by the neck until "Dead, Dead, Dead."

Among those brought to justice were Belle Starr, Cherokee Bill, the Dalton Gang, and others.

Belle Starr

Bringing in and arresting these desperadoes was a difficult task and sixty-five of Parker's officers died in the line of duty. One of the more famous characters associated with Parker is Rooster Cogburn, fictional character from the movie *True Grit*. The character Cogburn was based on the true life history of Cal Whitson, an actual deputy of the court. The young lady portrayed in the movie described herself as a resident of Dardanelle, Arkansas.

Many desperadoes and lawmen of national fame passed through or lived within the Arkansas River Valley. Belle Starr was known to have associates and family near Chickalah Mountain in Yell County and her husband Jim Reed had relatives that lived near Paris. She is reported to have traveled through down both the Old Military Road as well as the mail route through Reveille Valley on her way to visit relatives.

Wyatt Earp, famous as a lawman, was once arrested for minor theft in Van Buren. While awaiting trial, he escaped and fled west. In a short period of time, he showed up at railheads in Dodge City where he and his brothers became famous for taming the cowboys. Later, he took his talents to Tombstone, Arizona and he and his friends participated in the most famous shootout of all time at the OK Corral.

Wyatt Earp

After the Civil War, there were intermittent and sporadic clashes between former enemies but, by and large, the region was about as peaceful as it is today. Most crimes were minor in nature and usually involved disagreements over property lines or minor theft. Arguments that lead to death were virtually non-existent and, when one did occur, it became the talk of the region.

No crime and punishment occurring in the region has been more discussed and cussed than that involving the death of young Amanda Stephens and the subsequent trial of Arthur Tillman. The story contains every element of a dime-store novel. A young girl, product of a motherless family, is found dead in a deserted dug well near the small community of Delaware, Arkansas.

Amanda Stephens

John A. Tillman

Suspects abound and include her handsome boyfriend, jealous lovers, and perhaps even family members.

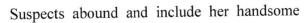

141

Nineteen-year old Amanda Stephens disappeared on March 10, 1913. Young Amanda had been living with her family which consisted of her father and several brothers. After the death of her mother, she was given the task of housekeeper and all of its accompanying chores and was known to be unhappy with the role she was forced to play. Attractive and outgoing, she had dated several young men in the community and was rumored to have been involved in one or more affairs. Her latest beau was young Arthur Tillman, the son of local farmer John F. Tillman. A note was found attached to her pillow which indicated she was "running away." When her father began searching for her, immediate suspicion was that she had "ran off" with Arthur. Her father sought and was issued a warrant for Tillman's arrest under the charge of seduction.

On March 18, local farmer Ambrose Johnson, who had been away from home for a few days, returned to find a dug well on his property had the edge caved in. Looking into the well, he found it was partially filled in with rocks. Curious, he began to remove rocks uncovering the body of Stephens. She had a bullet hole through her head and a telephone wire attached to a rock encircling her neck. An autopsy of the body revealed that young Amanda was four months pregnant.

The boyfriend, Arthur Tillman was the natural suspect and investigators began to collect further evidence that could be used against him during the trial. Evidence indicated that the murder had occurred in a nearby cabin, that Stephens had been shot in the head from above with a .22 caliber rifle, and that the body had been dumped into the well and covered with a wagon load of stone. Her hands grasped a fistful of dirt which indicated that she was not dead when deposited into the well.

Neighbors repeated stories and a rumor about Tillman including that he was seen sneaking around in the neighborhood where the body was found. His mother also assisted the prosecution

Sleepy Village of Paris, AR. 1900

by telling that Arthur possessed a .22 caliber rifle. Arthur was found at his uncle's house in Knoxville but escaped from the local police. He was eventually located in Fort Smith and arrested by Sheriff Cook of Johnson County and returned to Paris for trial.

Tillman was tried twice for the murder: the first trial, which began on August 27, 1913, ended with a hung jury. After his trial, Tillman was remanded to the state penitentiary while awaiting retrial. Tillman escaped again, this time jumping from a moving train in Perry County. He was recaptured ten hours later, hobbled and with two sprained ankles. When questioned about his escape attempt, Tillman blurted, "I wasn't trying to escape, I just wanted to kill myself."

Murder site, Johnson Home

Tillman was retried in October of 1913. Trial notes (a copy of which is located in the Logan County museum) indicate witness who swore adamantly that he was innocent while others swore just as vigorously that he was guilty. Tillman's primary defense was that Amanda was known to have had affairs with other men and that one of these people was the guilty party. Earl Bolden, one of Stephen's relatives and a married man, was believed by Tillman to be the guilty party.

Other witnesses also indicated that Amanda's father Green Stephens may have killed her out of anger or even that Tillman's father was the guilty party.

Tillman was pronounced guilty in November of 1913 and sentenced to die on the anniversary of the death of Amanda Stephens. Again sent to the state penitentiary, Tillman attempted his third escape. About five miles out of Paris, the train slowed to go up a slight grade. With chains and handcuffs around his arms and fetters on his feet, Tillman delivered a powerful kick which broke the chain about his ankles. Before his guards could stop him, he rushed to the car door and prepared to jump. Pausing for a second to check his surrounding before jumping resulted in his recapture and ended any chance he had for escape.

As months dragged on, Tillman and his family sought clemency from Governor Hayes. His affidavit to the governor offered this excuse for his sentence:

"I would make this statement again, and swear to it, if I had only one more minute to live, and all on God's earth I ask of you, your excellency, is that you give me a fair impartial investigation of my case, something I know I did not have, nor could have gotten at my trial, on account of strong prejudice against me in Logan County."

Obviously many people agreed with him. The governor received more than one-thousand

Paris Livery, 1914, just down the street from the execution site.

requests for clemency for the young man. Returned to Paris, Tillman awaited his final sentence while jailed in the Logan County jail. Rumors ran rampant throughout the community. According to various stories, Tillman's father had purchased a high-powered rifle which he was going to use to either shoot Arthur before he could be hanged or was going to use to assist him in his escape. The story of his last few hours is a poignant and sad story, a well-written story repeated from Sonya Fletchers 1964 story, *The Last Hanging in Arkansas.*

On July 13, 1914, holding him at arm's length the better to see his face, Mrs. J.F. Tillman bade

farewell that afternoon to her son Arthur, condemned to die. Neither mother nor son expected to

see each other alive again.

"My son," the mother sobbed as she looked through tears dimmed eyes,
"my little boy. You were never sweeter or dearer to your mother than you are today. I'll always know you are innocent,"
and unable to restrain herself, the mother flung her arms about Arthur's neck.
Every person in the penitentiary hospital who witnessed this event realized that, unless some

unforeseen interference prevented the execution, they had just witnessed the final goodbye

between mother and beloved son. Arthur attempted to comfort his mother but to no avail.

Mr. Ray, the Methodist circuit rider was with Tillman during his last hours. The only comment

offered up by Tillman was of his innocence.

"Arthur, for God's sake," said the minister, *"tell the whole truth right now. Are you innocent or guilty? I want to know if you are guilty so I may pray and have you join me in sincere prayer for forgiveness. If you are innocent, I want to hear the whole truth."*
"I am innocent," was the young man's reply, uttered in a firm tone of voice.

"But," the minister said, *"Suppose you are not telling the truth. Are you going to die with that*

thing on your head?"

"Brother Ray," said Tillman, *"I am not guilty. If I should confess to that crime when I did not do*

it, I would die with a lie on my lips. You don't want me to die that way, do you?"

"The courts condemned you," continued the minister, *"and everything is against you. Can you*

produce proof of you innocence? Is there not

something you can say at the last minute? If

you are innocent, who is the man?"

Scene at the jail as the execution approaches

45

Then Tillman mentioned the name of a relative of the murdered girl. He tried to shift the blame on him at the trial, but failed to furnish convincing proof. *"How do you know that man is guilty?"* said Ray.

"He was the first man to meet the girl," answered Tillman. *"Why, once he proposed to me that I swap Amanda Stevens to him for his wife. I would not do it, and then he told me one day that he was going to kill her."*

"Arthur," said the circuit minister, *"that is a mighty serious thing for you to say if you have no proof."*

"I can't help it; I can tell you nothing else. I am innocent," answered Tillman wringing his hands.

"I want to impress on you that you embrace religion and then make a false statement, you are in danger of going to hell," stated the minister.

"I can't help it, I tried to tell all at the court and they would not let me," wailed Tillman.

Several pathetic scenes took place when relatives of the boy called to bid him goodbye, but throughout it all it seemed that the lad's thoughts were of his mother and two little sisters. His last night on earth was sleepless and he failed to eat the chicken supper Sheriff Cook had especially provided. At one o'clock he asked members of the death watch for watermelon. This was secured and he ate ravenously. He afterwards requested that he be allowed to sleep until four o'clock and laid down, but rest was broken and he was awaken before the appointed time.

Logan County Museum, site of Hanging

When Sheriff Cook called at the jail, the boy's condition seemed to be weaker and one of the physicians told the sheriff that the boy would have to be given morphine. This was done and Sheriff Cook told Ray that the services would have to be held in the death cell. At the request of Tillman the minister sang "Shall we gather at the River" and "God be with You Till we Meet Again". In both these songs Tillman joined. Afterwards he told the minister he wanted to pray, in a voice of emotion he said"

"I know my time for this earth is short. I am being taken away while I am a young man. I can't grow up to take care of my good old mother. Oh Lord, I know she is crying for me now. Oh Lord, I wish I could be with her and I know you are with me. And then my two little sisters--look after them when I am gone, Oh Lord. Let them grow up to be good little girls. I am prepared to go. I believe strongly in salvation and repentance. My master told me I might be saved if I throw myself on the mercy of the court. So to thou mercy I throw myself on thee and cling, but I ask thee also not to forget those I love here on earth. I love everybody and I forgive everybody. I do not want to leave any enemies on earth."

After the prayer Tillman said to Sheriff Cook, *"I'm ready, but you will have to carry me."* It is not known whether this was intended as a threat of defiance or a reference to his physical condition. Without regard to the intent of the remark, Sheriff Cook motioned to his deputies. Wayne Cook and Sam Kincannon took Tillman by the arms and the march began. When he reached the scaffold, Tillman turned to the waiting crowd and said: *"I*

Tillman being escorted to execution

147

want everybody here when I am gone away to read the twenty-fifth verse of the twenty-seventh chapter of Deuteronomy. It says, 'Cursed be that taketh reward to slay and innocent person.'"

Afterward Arthur asked permission to pray a last prayer which was granted and he said: *"After I am gone, I ask Oh Lord to show mercy to those who have persecuted me. I ask that you be merciful to those who did not treat me right."*

"I love Judge Evans," cried Tillman. *"I love everybody. God knows I love everybody. Lord*

Gallows at Tillman Hanging

forgive this sheriff if this is an unjust step he is taking. Bless those who are going to kill me. I know I haven't long on this little platform where I am kneeling. Soon the trap door will spring and then death will claim me. When that takes place, Lord, I ask thee to take me by the river where we shall gather."

"Lord I am making a long prayer. It's hard to die so young. It's hard to leave my dear old mother. I know my mother will fill an early grave, Lord. She is too worried over this, and when she fills that early grave, I want those people to see that her body is buried by mine for I love my mother and my mother loves me. I ask thee again to watch over my little sisters and consecrate them to the Lord Jesus Christ and let them grow up to be good women. There isn't anything more I ask except I commend my soul to the care of the Lord. Amen."

After the prayer Sheriff Cook, in a trembling voice, read the death warrant and the ropes and straps were adjusted. He (Tillman) then asked someone to wipe the perspiration from his face and his uncle stepped forward. *"Thanks Uncle Jim,"* said the youth. *"Tell Mama I'm certainly going to Heaven this morning."*

At the site of the black cap, Tillman said, *"Goodbye people."* The cap was adjusted, Sheriff Cook stepped back, pulled the trigger, and the boy shot down. This ended hanging in the State of Arkansas.

Amanda Stephens

During the time between trial and execution, Arkansas passed a law

Tillman lead to execution

stating that all subsequent death penalties would be conducted by electric chair. Since the law came into effect after the Tillman trail was complete, the state proceeded with the hanging even though an electric chair sat in Little Rock ready for use.

One hundred years has elapsed since the death of young Amanda Stephens.

A new county court house has been erected, the old jail closed and converted to the Logan County museum. The old gallows were dismantled and became part of a barn located on the old Military Road. During that period, countless hours have been spent arguing the innocence or guilt of

Reenactment at Logan County Museum

the various parties involved. Advocates on one side claim that jail house confessions by Tillman clearly show he was guilty, opponents claim just as heatedly that the crime was committed by an another amorous lover or angry family member. Gail Ball, the granddaughter of Ambrose Johnson, now lives near her grandfather's property where Amanda's body was found. Ball was born in the same room where her grandmother and great-aunt cleaned Amanda's decomposing body before the autopsy was performed.

"I don't think Arthur did it," said Ball, who said she grew up with family talking about the case. "I grew up hearing about the story. We grew up knowing it. The land is still here in my family."

The Logan County museum reenacts the hanging on several occasions each year. Paris mayor Daniel Rogers replaces young John Tillman and marches up the thirteen steps of the gallows where he is meet by Sheriff James Hatcher and executioner Gene Davis. Jeanne S. Reynolds, proprietor of the museum, sings a ballad about the incident while other ladies dressed in costumes of the era add to the atmosphere by crying and calling out to the condemned. One-hundred years later, it is still a scene of sadness. Two young people, many family members, and people in the county lives were forever changed by these tragic events.

The main storyline still remains; Guilty or Innocent?

Paris at turn of Century

Loud Talkers, Dunkers, and Holy Rollers

Churches and religious faith have always been an important facet of life for people in the Shadow of the Mountain. Presbyterian, Methodist, and Baptist missionaries were some of the first people to move into the region. Many of these arrived to minister to the Indian population years before white man arrived in the area. Dwight Mission was established just west of Russellville to convert and educate the Cherokee

Established in 1820, it eventually became a small town with grist mill, sawmill, school, and various business. By 1828, the Cherokee had been removed to Oklahoma and settlers had begun to flood into the region.

Native Americans often named the various denominations by their most noticeable aspects. The Methodists- known at that time for their fiery demeanor and sermons were called the Loud Talkers. Baptists were known as the dunkers because they practiced immersion baptism.

The roles of these denominations were discussed earlier and, by the turn of the 19th century, a new movement, the Pentecostals, swept into the region. The largest of these "Full Gospel" groups were the Assembly of God but they also included Pentecostal Church of God, Jesus Only, Holiness, and the Apostolic Church of God. The Pentecostal movement began as an outgrowth of a 1906 revival on Azusa Street, Los Angeles, California. Emphasizing spiritual gifts including healing and speaking in tongues, the Pentecostals saw themselves as the third Great Awakening of the Protestant faith. By

1912, they were conducting revival services in Russellville, Paris, Booneville,

Greenwood, and in many of the small communities in the

area. The Assembly of God denomination was formed

during a 1916 meeting held near the Mountain Valley

water headquarters in downtown Hot Springs. The Rev.

E.R. Fitzgerald preached throughout the region and

established many of the churches that became charter

E. R. Fitzgerald

members of the Assemblies of God. These included the

churches at Russellville, Midway, and Paris. Many of the early ministers and

missionaries for the denomination were men from the mountain communities.

Early revival meetings were often held in brush arbors or outdoors during the summer

time after the crops were planted and growing. A speaker would arrive in the area, set up

a stage, and services would be held nightly during meeting that would go far into the

night. These nightly services would sometimes continue for weeks and would attract

people from throughout the region. Many people came out of religious zeal while others

came to watch. Many of the older boys and men would remain outside the arbor during

the meetings and would spend their time smoking, gossiping, and sometimes even

passing the bottle around the group. Pentecostal services were exciting- new gospel

songs were sang with accompanying music from guitars, piano's, hand clapping and

much enthusiasm. This was followed by preaching- loud passionate preaching

accompanied by dramatic movement and prayer. Calls to the altar resulted in tears of

passion and rejoicing and speaking in "tongues." Overcome by the word, people would often jump in joy or run around the encampment, much to the delight of the onlookers. Derisive terms of Holy Roller, Pew Jumpers, and worse were ascribed to the believers. In Midway, the Lasaster's, Parson's, and Wright's were some of the first to become involved with the new church. In 1912, a group of the locals meet and built the first church; located just south of highway 22 on Sorghum Hollow Road. The frame building stood for many years before finally catching on fire and burning to the ground in the 60's. After the church moved to its present site, my grandfather Lee bought the building and used it as a home for many years.

Other small churches were being built in the small communities found on both sides of the mountain. These included churches in St. Louis Valley, Magazine, Union, Greasy Valley, Booneville, and Paris.

Many of the churches faced local opposition and were a source of fun for the young men of the community. While young, Arve and Ravlin Davison decided to have fun at the expense of the local holiness. Revival services had been going on for weeks and all the young ladies in the area were in church and things were slow. During the day, the two filled a bottle with large red wasps and inserted a rag into the mouth to keep the beasts in captivity. That night, revival services were being conducted at the old frame church just down the road. The building, built of rough pine lumber, set high off the ground on piles of sandstone rock. The back of the church, where the preaching platform was located, was probably two foot or more off the red clay surface. The rough pine had dried and several knots in the wood had fallen out, leaving holes where the two brothers could observe what was going on within the building. The two sat through the singing and preaching, waiting until just the right moment during the altar service. Finally, soaked in sweat from the hard preaching, the minister gave the altar call and dozens flocked to the front for prayer. Shaking the bottle, the boys could hear the angry stirring and feel the vibration of the insects within the jar. Pulling the lid from the jar, they inserted the mouth into the missing pine knot and released the critters into the building. The irate insects swarmed into the crowd and immediately began to exact what they perceived as justice to their captors. Girls screamed, older women began to jump about, and the men began to wave their arms as they swatted. The minister, convinced that revival was on the way, began to shout louder and louder as the music played. Finally, overcome by repeated stings, one of the young ladies realized the cause of the excitement, screamed "red wasps," and beat a hasty exit out the back door. She was soon joined by the entire congregation. The two young culprits rolled from beneath the church and disappeared into the darkness.

Dry, hot summers and drought conditions caused great suffering among the many farmers in the region. Totally reliant upon good weather and rainfall for their survival,

155

congregations would hold prayer services and plead for abundant rainfall. During one of these periods, young men from St. Louis Valley contrived a method to grant the pastor his wishes. On the day prior to the service, they constructed a device that would dump a large pail of water. Climbing into the half-loft above the stage, they filled the bucket to

Gorman and Imogene Daniel, 1940

capacity with water from Shoal Creek. Just as the pastor implored God for rain and looked pleadingly toward the ceiling, they pulled the string and dumped several gallons of rain onto the unsuspecting minister's head. For years, various members of the community were blamed for the pastor baptizing. On another occasion, Clyde Daniel of the Cabin Creek community decided to disrupt services by playing cowboy during the service. Waiting until the service was in full swing, he rode his horse into the back door of the building, whooped as he galloped down the central aisle, and escaped through the side door. The service continued. Both Clyde and his brother Gorman became Assembly of God ministers and served God faithfully for many years.

Water baptisms were commonly held throughout the county. With their strong belief in total immersion under water, many of the local churches held baptism services at local streams. The congregants would gather on the stream bank, waiting for the special services. Surviving an Arkansas baptism alone was an act of faith. The pastor stumbled over wet leaves, slippery rocks, and debris until chest deep in the water, followed by those to be baptized. Many aspirants tumbled into the frigid waters and baptized themselves numerous times before arriving at the proper site. Nevertheless, once there, the minister grappled the candidate into position, blessed them in the name of the Father, Son, and Holy Ghost and deposited them backward into the stream. The cold water and shock of immersion was enough to take ones breath. Watching some of the coal miners and various other former miscreants emerge from the water was often too much for the faithful and family on shore. Some would have a run-away and race up and down the bank in praise of God while others jumped into the stream to welcome the newly baptized. Entire afternoons were devoted to the exercise and the accompanying dinner on the grounds.

Baptism at railroad hole on Short Mountain Creek, Paris, AR.

Music was an important facet of many of the churches attended by Scotch-Irish descendants. Not only were the traditional instruments of organ and piano used, churches included the drums, tambourine, guitar, bass, mandolin, and other stringed instruments. Scotch-Irish likes nothing more than a ballad, especially one containing some element of sadness or strife. Add a bluesy sound, a lot of instrumentation, a little hardship and tribulation, and you have the beginning of the country music. Many of the stars of country music are of Scotch-Irish background and began their singing careers within the church. Those include Elvis Presley, Loretta Lynn, Jerry Lee Lewis, and Johnny Cash.

Many people in the Shadow of the Mountain were musically inclined or, if they couldn't sing, loved to listen to good music. Each year, Logan and surrounding counties would hold a singing convention

Midway Trio-Mary Horne, Dale Foster, Margie Trusty

and churches from across the region would meet, practice, and demonstrate their musical talent. In between conventions and revivals, people would meet at community buildings or in neighbor's yards to play and sing. Various talented groups toured the area, singing and playing at churches. Midway Assembly of God always had a quartet of girls that sang at churches, the Singing Robinson family of Greasy Valley toured, and the Steffy Family wrote and recorded several gospel albums. Bob Wootton was talented enough that he played with Johnny Cash and the Tennessee

Johnny Cash and Bob Wootton

Three and was part of one of Cash's biggest performances ever when he played lead guitar at San Quentin Prison live. On several occasions, Hootenanny's were held on the square at Paris and various groups would come out to perform. For years, County Line Sale barn has carried on this tradition by hosting singing in the sale arena every Wednesday morning.

158

The tradition continues. Recently, we were invited to attend a Saturday evening fish fry and singing at the Methodist Church in Blue Ball. Everyone in the community showed up, many bringing musical instruments or carrying old hymnals from the various area churches. Sitting outside on the church grounds, everyone enjoyed a community dinner and then gathered around the picnic area for music lead by the Millard family. People in the audience called out a book and page number, the congregation would turn to the music and sing along accompanied by various guitars, bass, mandolin, and violin. On occasion, players would change instruments or a new arrival would join in the band. Talented singers demonstrated their talents as the audience clapped their hands and tapped feet to the rhythm.

Many outstanding ministers and church leaders originated in the various valleys and hollows of Magazine Mountain. Two of the best known were the Hutchison brothers, Fay and Alfred. Both men were well educated and well known in national theological

Fay Hutchinson

circles. Alfred was guest speaker and presenter at several of the Ivy League theological centers including Princeton University in New Jersey. He taught at religious colleges for several years before pastoring various small churches including Greasy Valley A/G. Reverend Fay Hutchison pastored several churches and then served as district Presbyter (director) of the Arkansas Assembly of God from 1965-1976.

During this time, the small denomination that had begun in the Shadow of the Mountain in the early 1900's had grown to thousands of churches and over 15 million members worldwide.

Churches, both Protestant and Catholic, have served as the catalyst for the community. Church revivals, dinners, singing conventions, and weekly meetings bring people of the community together and unite them in common endeavors. Many of the early schools were held in church buildings and were often taught by ministers. The Catholic community formed their own schools and seminaries at St. Scholastica, Subiaco Academy, St. Josephs, and other parochial schools have long provided educational and religious training to their church members.

Many stories about Catholic education could be recounted by members of the community. One of the most entertaining involved Gerhard Nehus, one of my former students. Gerhard is and was quite mischievous and had been disciplined by the sister's on several occasions. While on the playground, he and a friend determined to get even by placing sand in the gas tank of the schools vehicle. Within days, the vehicle was having mechanical difficulty and the two boys became very worried about their sins. Gerhard determined that the only way out of his predicament was total confession. Going into the confessional, Gerhard had a seat and whispered through the window, "Father, forgive me for I have sinned." No doubt, the priest had heard that voice on several occasions; especially when the child was sent to his office for discipline. "Continue, my son, he replied. "I placed sand in the gas tank," replied the recalcitrant youth. Immediately there was a commotion on the other side of the booth and the priest rounded the corner, securing a firm hold on the young man's shoulder. "I should have known it was you. Now, who else was with you? Be quick about it," demanded the priest in a stern voice. Scared into compliance, Gerhard gave up the name of his companion. Needless to say, more than a few Hail Mary's was exacted for the young men's redemption.

Dozens of Cumberland Presbyterian, Baptist, Methodist, Church of Christ, and others are scattered across the country side. On Sunday mornings, church bells peal across the valleys, calling the faithful to worship and prayer.

As long as people of a region share a basic core of beliefs, faith, language, and values we will always have a strong community and nation and the backbone of all of that is the Church.

St. Benedicts Mobile Wagon Church

Arkansas Treasure

Perhaps because of the poverty found in rural areas of Arkansas or because of the Scotch-Irish gift of gab, stories abound of treasure hidden in the Ozarks. Some of these stories have merit but no substantial amount of gold or silver has ever been located.

The stories begin with the journeys of Hernado De Soto into the Mississippi Valley and up the Arkansas River in 1541-42. His primary goal was to establish Spanish claims on the explored territories and to seize any gold and silver that he could locate. While crossing the Arkansas delta region, de Sota heard of great deposits of gold to be found in the mountains to the west. He first journeyed into the Ozarks but failed to find gold in the Batesville region. Turning south, he traveled searching for the Cayas Indian tribe. The Cayas were located in the River Valley region, probably centered in the Carden Bottoms of Yell County. De Soto and his men traveled further up the river before turning and exploring mountains around present day Fort Smith.

Stories of De Soto's gold abound throughout the region. Many swear the gold in buried in a defile on Magazine Mountain while others point to sites on Rich Mountain near Mena, Poteau Mountain, and other sites.

One of the more compelling stories involves the Old Spanish Mine near Turner Bend. Whether the gold is from De Soto or some latter group of Spanish is not clear but the general story states that a group of Spanish brought a galleon up the Arkansas and thence to a site on the Mulberry River near present day Turner Bend. The Spanish had heard stories of immense wealth mined from silver deposits in the area.

Obtaining gold and silver in abundance from local mines worked by the natives, the Spanish buried a huge portion of it in one of the mines, hoping to return for the treasure at some future point. They then sailed downstream in their galleon, obviously during

flood stage because the galleon is thought to have sunk. In fact, according to several

local residents, during the flood of 1927 several people observed the dragon bow of the

boat exposed just south of present-day Cass. The 1927 flood

was of historic proportions and covered much of the state. The

current and depth of the Mulberry was so large, no-one could

investigate and the ship had disappeared by the time the water

subsided.

The story of the lost mine was repeated throughout the region.

Around the turn of the century, Dr. Tobe Hill, a doctor in the

town of Mulberry, became infatuated with the story- so much

so that the quit his practice and devoted twenty years of his

Drawings near Cass, Arkansas

live and a small fortune in searching for the gold.

Dr. Hill was sure that the gold was located in a cliff found about five miles above Turner

Bend. The cliff was composed of a soft-grainy siltstone composed of red hematite

sandwiched between layers of limestone. Ancient markings abound on the cliff wall and

obviously predate settlers or even the more recent Cherokee. The siltstone is soft and

easily removed and evidence of diggings abound.

Dr. Hill purchased the land from George Washington Turner for the price of $750. He

was unable to find the opening to a large mine but became convinced that the many

Indian carvings held the key to its location. Dr. Hill traveled to the West, looking for

help. He located and hired a Pueblo Indian named Mexican Charley to return with him to

interpret the markings. Charley was placed in charge of the mining crew.

The news of Charley's arrival spread through the neighborhood and large crowd of people gathered to watch. Dr. Hill felt it necessary to hire men with guns to keep the crowds of people back as his miners worked.

Elias Russell

People throughout the county became excited when it was announced that Charley had found the location of the cap rock. So sure was he of success, Dr. Hill applied to the state for police protection for his treasure.

A huge and excited crowd gathered for the event. People milled around for hours, waiting on Mexican Charley to arrive. Charley, fearful of failure and afraid of what the crowd might do to him, remained in hiding. Before the ending of the day, it became necessary to provide Charley protection from the angry mob. He was given instruction to leave the country and to never return.

Elias Russell lived within three miles of the mine all his life. He hauled lumber from his sawmill to the mine and was deputy sheriff twenty-two years during the mining

operation. It was Mr. Russell who protected Mexican Charley from the hands of the mob. "Interest in the mine was high here and everywhere then," he said. "Women, as far away as Dallas, Texas, sold their feather beds for money to buy the mining stock, and lots of people would buy it again if it got started again. I always thought the place was just an old Indian village site and what they found were Indian bones and trinkets."

Others, including area resident Sarah Arbuckle, swore that the mine area was seeded with ore from Joplin, Missouri to increase the value of the stock. She bought some shares herself "But never got anything out of it," she declared.

Later, a man named Joseph Palmer came to the mine. Meeting Dr. Hill, he swore he could locate gold by witching with a pronged stick. He demonstrated his ability using a stack of silver, gold, and copper coins. Dr. Hill devised a test by hiding coins around the property. Palmer was able to locate several of the coins but stated that the gold in the mine was diverting his ability. Hill refused to let him search further.

Dr. Hill kept thirty men working eight hour per day shifts over a period of several years. He paid laborers five dollars per day- big wages for the time period. To fund this, he sold shares of his mine throughout the region. He sold at least 232 shares at a price of from $25- $100 per share and spent the money in his efforts. He died still expecting to find the gold.

Author at Mining Site

The mine has drifted into and out of operation several times since that date. The last to own and operate the mine were G. W. Glaze and his wife, from Salt Lake City. He was a prospector and artist-sign painter. Both he and his wife mined for the gold. Mrs. Glaze died in their cabin near the mine, from a heart attack, about three years ago. Soon after her death, Mr. Glaze left as suddenly as he had appeared, apparently abandoning everything, and has not been heard from since.

Today, the mine is located in a cove on the north side of

the Mulberry River. Large cliffs featuring tumbled talus slopes and overhanging ridges break up perpendicular cliffs. The cove itself is about a quarter mile long and a few hundred yards wide and is bisected by Cove Creek. The family living on-site operates a small saw mill and farm and entertains a few tourists who happen by. Beside their home, the cliff face is covered with modern and ancient graffiti and interlaced with tunnels running back into the mountain. Seven of the tunnels are large enough for small donkey-drawn cars to haul out debris collected within the mine. The tunnels are assessable but are filled with muddy water, some as much as twenty-feet deep. While few visit, locals still discuss the treasure and where it might be located.

 Other lost Spanish sites include several stories of caves on Magazine, Rich, and even Huckleberry Mountain. Many of these stories were embellished in telling and added to by local pranksters who etched treasure related graffiti on stone. Many of these are more than one-hundred years old which makes it difficult to know what is and isn't authentic. A recent stone found on Huckaberry has the carving, De Soto.

The rock is huge and oddly shaped and has other names inscribed as well. My grandparents, Lee and Nettie have their names carved into Buzzard Rock, the cliff near the De Soto stone as do many others. One of the Rollans family names is dated in the 1880's.

De Soto and other Spanish and French explorers wondered around the region for more than two-hundred years prior to English settlement. The names they assigned places are still very much a part of the Arkansas landscape. We have the Fouche LaFave River, Petit Jean Mountain and River, Ozark (Big Arc), Lavaca (the cow), Vache Grasse (Fat Cow), and dozens of other locations that mark their existence. As for De Soto, his journey ended in starvation and death for him and many of his followers. His journey could be looked upon as a failure, the stories of great wealth told by the local Indian tribes led to further exploration by the Spanish and to some great stories for local treasure hunters.

A more plausible treasure story centers on Arkansas, the Civil War, and a group known as the Knights of the Golden Circle. The Knights of the Golden Circle (K.G.C.) were a secretive organization created in 1854, proposed to establish a slaveholding empire encompassing the southern United States, the West Indies, Mexico, and parts of Central America. The empire was expected to center on Havana, Cuba and would consist of a circle of states 2,500 in diameter which accounts for the name. The K.G.C. would be a plantation based society and would hold a virtual monopoly on tobacco, sugar, and cotton. They also supported the continuance of slavery to support this society.

George W. L. Bickley, a Virginia-born doctor, editor, and adventurer, was the leader and creator of the organization. His imaginary country consisted of states controlled by local "castles" or chapters formed in cities such as Houston, San Antonio, and other key locations.

Newspapers across the South reacted favorably to his message and several noted individuals joined his organization.

As the Civil War approached, the organization picked up members and steam. Mexico, facing political unrest, was one of the first targets of the organization. Bickley attempted to organize a coup of the country in 1860 but he felled to gather enough members in New Orleans to attempt the invasion.

The K.G.C. had an elaborate set of rituals, codes, signs, and passwords. They organized into groups of Knights who were in charge of military, commercial, financial, or political affairs. These were divided into two groups; the foreign and home guards. The foreign guards were responsible for participating in the overthrow of regional countries while the home guard worked within the U.S. At its peak, the K.G.C were said to have more than sixteen thousand members.

During the Civil War, it gained popularity with many of the officers of the Confederacy,

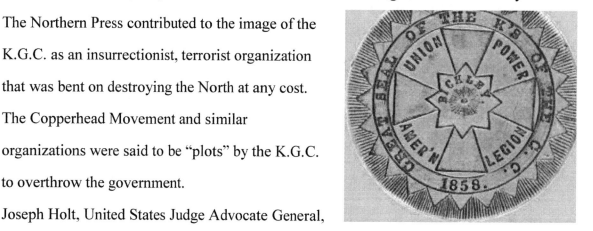

especially those caught up in the Sir Walter Scott vision of knighthood and chivalry.

The Northern Press contributed to the image of the K.G.C. as an insurrectionist, terrorist organization that was bent on destroying the North at any cost. The Copperhead Movement and similar organizations were said to be "plots" by the K.G.C. to overthrow the government.

Joseph Holt, United States Judge Advocate General,

submitted a report in October 1864 that warned Secretary of War Edwin Stanton about the danger of this plot, which he attributed at times to the K.G.C. and at other times to different treasonous groups.

Perhaps the best documentation as to the power and influence of the Knights of the Golden Circle during the Civil War is *The Private Journal and Diary of John H. Surratt, The Conspirator* which was written by John Harrison Surratt and later edited by Dion Haco and published by Frederic A. Brady of New York in 1866. In this journal, Surratt goes into great detail when describing how he was introduced to the K.G.C. in the summer of 1860 by another Knight, John Wilkes Booth, and inducted into this mysterious organization on July 2, 1860, at a castle in Baltimore, Maryland. Surratt describes the elaborate and secret induction ceremony and its rituals and tells that cabinet members, congressmen, judges, actors, and other politicians were in attendance. Maybe the most significant revelation of Surratt's diary is that the Knights of the Golden Circle began plotting to kidnap Abraham Lincoln in 1860, before Lincoln was even inaugurated in 1861, and continued throughout the Civil War, resulting in President Lincoln's assassination by fellow Knight Booth on April 14, 1865.

According to many of the stories associated with the K.G.C., the organization realized

General JO Shelby

that the North would prevail and began to make contingencies for that event. Military men within the organization were prepared to escape to other countries, taking men, supplies, and money with them to make this possible. According to this theory, millions of dollars were removed from the treasury in Richmond as well as other locations and was secreted in sites around the U.S. Other "home guard" was instructed to obtain money through deceit, theft, and corruption and to hold it until "the South Could Rise Again."

General Joseph Shelby, Frank and Jessie James, the Younger brothers, and others are thought to be members of the K.G.C. Rumors abound that these men and others were involved in the plot to keep the Confederacy alive. Money was shifted to the Western theater during the war and these men and others secreted it away. Large amounts of arms and bullion were hidden in scattered locations and marked by secret symbols that only other members could recognize. General Shelby, famous for his "Great Raid" into Missouri in 1863 as well as other notable exploits, refused to surrender at the conclusion of the Civil War. Pursued by Union troops under General Sherman, he and over one-thousand men crossed into Mexico at Eagle Pass, Texas. It was first assumed that he would overthrow Emperor Maximillian and assist the Mexicans in reestablishing a

government that was sympathetic to the Southern cause. For whatever reason, this did not occur and Shelby eventually returned to the U.S. Jessie and Frank James, along with the Coles and Youngers, robbed and pillaged throughout the mid-west, accumulating huge amounts of wealth in the process. Former Confederate officer and Shelby adjunct John Edwards made heroes of the entire group, writing

Johnathan Newman Edwards

story after story of their exploits while editor serving as editor of a Kansas City newspaper. General John Sappington Marmaduke, commander of Cavalry in Arkansas, returned to Missouri and eventually became governor of the state.

General John Marmaduke

All of these men were rumored to be K.G.C. and all had amazing success or, in the case of the outlaws, fame after the war. All are rumored to have been involved in secreting wealth for the Confederacy and in an interest in reviving the South. Only toward the latter part of his life did General Shelby renounce his former actions and settle down to the aristocratic life he had previously enjoyed prior to the war.

All of these are involved in the story of hidden gold in the Ozarks. General Jo Shelby was a native of Missouri and a planter. He became a very successful Confederate General and was eventually given control of all forces west of the Mississippi after the conclusion of the war. His commanding officer is General Marmaduke and both knew and were closely associated with the James brothers and other notorious outlaws. In fact, General Shelby was rescued at Prairie Groove by none other than Frank James and both of the James boys were known to have ridden with his troops.

Did this group hide money in the Ouachita's in hope of recreating the Confederacy? Many think the possibility exists. Rumors have abounded for years that a weapons cache is buried on Magazine Mountain and near Cox Valley. At Cox Valley, natives point at a great slab of rock that has fallen across the cliff face and became jammed tightly against the cliff. Marks at the top of the cliff clearly indicate wedge marks where the rock was worked and then tumbled down the mountain. What is hidden beneath? Many people are curious enough that sums of money have been invested to remove the stone. So vast is the size of the rock, it cannot be budged even by modern equipment.

Even more compelling is the story that gold was hidden in the Ouachita's and clues were left in the rock that would indicate its recovery. In the book *Rebel Gold*, gold and silver from the Confederacy was hidden in a cave within the mountain system. For years, gold seekers have traversed around the community of Hatfield, rumored to be the site for the treasure.

The clues for where the gold was to be found are inscribed upon a rock

Inscribed rock found on Rich Mountain

The site was to be well hidden and located in a region that was not frequented by many individuals.

While exploring Rich Mountain, three large stones were uncovered. Located near Devils Backbone, these stone are isolated and, additionally are located on the side of a ridge on a small bench. Each stone is from five to perhaps twenty foot in length, several feet wide, and deeply buried into the earth.

Thinking we had discovered native Indian drawings, I contacted the state archelogist at Arkansas Tech University. His investigation indicated that the stone was probably etched in the 1800's and, though interesting, held little archeological evidence. After visiting the site a couple of times out of curosity, it was completely forgotten.

In 2011, Paris placed the sesquicentential Civil War marker at the Logan County fair grounds. The marker indicates where General Joseph Shelbys Iron Brigade fought a skirmish against the First Arkansas Infantry. Research indicated Shelby, an avowed K.G.C. member, traveled thought the area on his way to Missouri. His troop consisted of several local men who knew the country well enough that they lead him through Pleasant (Harkey) Valley, to Shoal Creek Mill in St. Louis Valley, and thus to the Old Military Road.

During research and while reading about Shelby, his involvment with the K.G.C. became evident. While reading *Rebels Gold*, I discovered the symbols for the hidden treasure was a bow and arrow, a turtle, and a map. Other evidence indicating K.G.C. involvement in the local area include:

1) Rumors that Confederate gold is hidden in the Ouachita Mountains.

2) Persistent local rumors that gold has been buried on Magazine.

3) General Joseph Shelby, an avowed leader in the K.G.C., is well-known in the area and has traveled within miles of the site on several occassions.

4) Three rocks bearing K.G.C. symbols are located in an isolated area. The rock carvings date, not from prehistoric time, but from the 1800's and possibly during the Civil War.

5) Marker trees and rocks found throughout the River Valley.

Several pieces of information all pointing to the same thing!!! Coincidence? Chance? Luck?

Several individuals have searched for this gold but, thus far, it has eluded discovery even thought K.G.C. treasure has been discovered in several other locations associated with the James boys and other member of the K.G.C.

Does other hidden treasure exist in the Ozarks and Ouachita's? During the Civil War many individuals hid their wealth in various locations including old mason jars that were inserted into the ground or into old fireplace mantel or bricks.

 In 2012, millions of dollars of old coins were found buried in the back yard of an individual living in San Francisco. Golden City, a community near Booneville, was the site of a gold rush around the turn of the century, and diamonds are extracted from the green Arkansas earth at Murfreesboro every year.

Even though people continually search for riches, the River Valley's true treasure is not the things that can be bought and sold. Our true treasure is our people, our culture, and the mountains and valleys in which we exist.

Shirley Motor Company 1936, Ford place

. Towns, Cities, and Wide Places in the Road

Crows circle in the distance, their mournful cawing and the tinkling of falling water the only sound disrupting the stillness of the forest. A young deer pauses from browsing and glances nervously about. Broken stone foundation and brick scatter the ground around the creek, testament to the forgotten community that once bustled along both banks. Now there is nothing but National Forest, a seldom used dirt road, and the creek crossed by a span of wooden timber.

Before the turn of the 20th century, Millard was a thriving town. Like many of the small towns built where running water was available to turn paddle wheels, Millard had a saw mill, a shake mill (used to make roofing), grist mill, store, and a nearby cotton gin.

The Lee, Valentine, White, and Rogers family lived on property nearby and people from the surrounding area and from on top of Magazine Mountain visited to receive mail, buy essentials such as sugar, coffee, tea, and other products that could not be grown locally. Millard was located on a major road which connected mail routes from Belleville, Danville, and Yell County across Green Bench into Logan and Franklin County.

Water tumbles from the near-by elevations of Magazine Mountain, enters Bear Gap hollow, and forms Shoal Creek. At Millard, the downward erosion of the stream was hindered by capstones of sandstone, forming a natural bridge that allowed passage of wagons and buggy's belonging to early pioneers.

It was a natural place for a small town to develop. The stream supplied water for animals and human alike and was a cheap source of energy to power equipment. Even before the Civil War, scattered farms were located on both sides of the stream.

The life of inhabitants of a region is determined by geography. This is especially true of the Arkansas River Valley. Running some seventy-five miles east to west and about twenty-miles from north to south, the valley bisect the Ozark Mountains to the north and the Ouachita Mountains to the south. The centerpiece of this region is the Arkansas

River and the flat bottom lands that edge it. Rich alluvial lands, these bottoms attracted early settlers who snapped the land up and developed a plantation system of life. People living in Roseville, Dardanelle, Ozark, and along the Petit Jean River in Yell, Polk, and South Logan County had

Millard Crossing

extensive farms, business, sometimes slaves, and were closely associated with life of the "Old South."

Moving further from the river, pioneers began to encounter parallel ridges of folded sandstone and shale. Of limited value, settlers looked for gaps or places where streams had eroded through these ridges and where roads could be constructed. Passing through the gaps allowed settlers access to the valleys between the ridges. Although the land was not as fertile, these lands were soon purchased and communities named after the pioneer

families developed. These included Ferguson Valley, Cox Valley, Dutch Creek, and St.

Louis Valley.

Proceeding toward the high peaks of Magazine, Petit Jean, Huckaberry, and Nebo are

stair-step areas of level land called benches or small, narrow valleys called hollows.

Although not high quality farm land, enough high land cotton, corn, and truck crops

could be grown to support a family. The land was cheaper, required intensive labor, and

was usually settled by Scotch-Irish settlers who eked out a living through hard work and

enterprise.

Many small communities, including Millard, developed within these nocks and crannies of the mountains. Prior to the Civil War, several families subsisted on upper Shoal Creek and on the benches of Nebo,

Chickalah, Rich, and Huckaberry Mountain. Of Union persuasion, many of them were

forced to join the Confederacy during the early years of the war or to vacate their homes

and hideout in mountain crannies as they avoided the Confederate home guard.

After the war, men who had fought for the South lost citizenship for a period of ten years

so the old "Feds" became the new power base. Families and towns that had once been

hotbeds of the Confederacy lost political power. In 1871, Booneville, the county seat of

Scott County, not only lost their county seat, but were moved into the newly concocted

Sarber County. Union veterans such as James Garner, James Laffery, Daniel R. Lee, and

"Wild Bill" Heffington

James A. Shrigley became the political leaders of the region. The latter three were chosen to select the new county seat. Their first choice was Revelee, a small community on the old post road to Booneville. Later they moved the county seat to the town of Ellsworth, a small town on the Military Road near present day Midway. The move was highly controversial and stirred up dissent across the county. After protest and burning of the courthouse, the county seat was eventually established in the middle of pasture land near Short Mountain and named Paris.

Joseph J. Rogers moved from Hamilton County, Tennessee and settled in the Millard Community in 1858. Soon after establishing a home, the Civil War began. His father, Henry joined the Union Army and was killed in Springfield, Missouri. Joseph and his

brothers became a part of the "Mountain Feds" and eventually joined the Arkansas First Infantry under the command of "Wild" Bill Heffington. Heffington's reputation was dubious. He had joined the Confederacy in Dardanelle in 1861 and then returned home after the defeat at Pea Ridge. He "enlisted" a group of more than one-hundred men and attacked Union forces near Indian Springs

Joseph J. Rogers

in Danville. A few weeks later, he attacked Confederate forces at Dardanelle and retreated to Magazine Mountain using the uniforms he obtained from the Federals he had killed.

In 1863, he led his group to Fayetteville where they joined the Union First Infantry. Edley, John, and Joseph Rogers joined along with him. All three lived near Millard in

Henry Mossengal

the Salem community. Neighbors who joined along with them included George Adams, Levi and George Fink, William Hawkins, and several of the Whites. After skirmishes in south-west Missouri, they returned to the Magazine Mountain area and established a headquarters at Blacksnake ridge on the south side of the mountain. A virtual redoubt with flat top and sides riddled with caves, the hideout served as a perfect hideout for guerrilla warfare. At least one pitched battle involving more than one-hundred men was fought as Confederates tried to raid the hide-out.

Several of the men, including Heffington, had a reward placed on their head. The amount for the capture or death of Heffington was $15,000. The extent of the Rogers involvement is not known but others, including Henry Mossengal, had to flee because of depredations committed during the war.

After the war, the industrious Rogers brothers became owners of a saw and a grist mill as well as a cotton gin. Several of the business in and around

Edley Jackson Rogers

Millard belonged to them and they had extensive property ownership in the area. They eventually expanded by adding a cotton gin near Belleville. By 1890, their plant was valued at $3,000. The cotton gin processed up to 600 bales of cotton per season,

Nathan Ellington, First Logan County Judge

most picked in the Petit Jean River valley. The lumber yard produced more than 5,000 board feet of lumber per day. Another prominent citizen of the community was Nathan Ellington. His family moved to Arkansas from Virginia, through Tennessee, and eventually to Chismville. He and his first wife had seven children before she passed away in 1857. A year later, he married Elvira Garner and they produced four more children.

Mr. Ellington was a prosperous farmer and community leader as the Civil War began. Although his family appears divided in loyalty, Mr. Ellington seems to have remained an ardent supporter of the Union. His son, Thomas Nathan Ellington married Martha Charlotte Metcalf of Chismville in 1860. He purchased eighty acres of land near Booneville in May of 1861. Apparently, he and two of his brothers were part of the Arkansas home guard. He enlisted as a private in the Caddo Rifles, Co. C, 4th Arkansas Infantry with his two brothers, George W. and William J. Ellington. The regiment was involved in protecting the frontier in Indian Territory and latter was involved in the battle of Pea Ridge on March 7-8, 1862. The group lost 55 of their 695 men at Pea Ridge. After the battle, the forces regrouped at Van Buren and then marched overland to Des Arc where they boarded a steamboat to Memphis. They arrived too late to participate in the battle of Shiloh so they were reassigned to a camp near Tupelo, Mississippi. Dozens of Arkansas soldiers died of disease in the camp hospital during this period of time. Many of the men had signed up for short-terms and were ready to leave when those terms were complete. Thomas Nathan was evidently one of these for the obtained his discharge on 6-21-1862.

Thomas must have returned home to utter confusion. Former neighbors were in arms against each other and guerilla fighters with changing allegiance roamed the hills and valleys of the River Valley. His father, a known unionist, was in a tenuous situation, surrounded by a home guard that was determined to maintain the Confederacy. Thomas' sister Martha Jane was married to Charles Pincney Anderson (his uncle was the famous Sam Houston who also supported the Union) who was a Captain in the Union Army. Two of the Metcalf's, Thomas N. brothers-in-law were also in the Union Army. All three, plus other relatives and friends, had joined the Union cause and the Confederate home guard was making their life difficult. Mary Jane was forced to hide food, animals, and personnel goods of any value to prevent the home guard from stealing. Relatives had to assist her and her large family to prevent starvation.

Other families in the region suffered equally from the actions of these men. Riding out in groups, the guerillas terrorized the region. Women hid money and valuable in fruit jars and buried them around their homes, food had to be stored in caves, and animals had to be hidden to prevent outright theft by the group. Families thought to be sympathetic to the Union cause were beaten to death, hanged, or shot by the home guard. Nathan, along with his brother Lewis and William switched sides and joined the Second Arkansas Infantry, USA. They enrolled as a private in company B on September 10, 1863 at Dardanelle, Arkansas. He eventually was promoted to corporal and, sometime

181

during his career, was severally wounded in his right leg. He suffered from this for the remainder of his life and, in 1889, received a pension from the U.S.

The primary duties of the Second Infantry were to protect the home front and to rid the country-side of the scalawags that were preying on the local population.

Nathan's brother William was a favorite of their commanding officer. The officer often used William as a scout to investigate local conditions. William moved rapidly into and out of the many valleys and hollows, picking up information from the women and

Thomas Nathan and Martha (Metcalf) Ellington

children sympathetic to the union. Women would indicate they had important messages by hanging sheets or colored clothing out to dry in a specific pattern. William watched from the hillside until he could get the message and safely deliver it to his commander. He and local Confederate commander Jim Sewell were in frequent conflict and developed a healthy respect for each other.

Without fear of any kind, William had many personal encounters with the lawless guerillas that frequented the hills. Whether obtaining the rank or just given the title, he became known as Captain William. He hunted down many of the thieves and robbers and dealt out swift justice to many of the worst kind of people. During this period and immediately after the war, there was a good deal of ill will between men who were involved in the war. William was able to make friends with Sewell after the war and both served on the Logan County Board of Commissioners. He was not so successful with other of his enemies and this ill will cost him his life.

For years after the war, William always carried a weapon to protect himself. In 1890, even after years of peaceful farming, William had enemies. He traveled into town carrying his weapon but left it in his buggy when going into a local store. Upon entering the store, his enemy drew a weapon and shot the defenseless William. Hearing gunfire, his son ran into the building and was also killed. His wife, Amanda Robison, and he had eleven children that they raised in Logan County.

Nathan was said to be one of the few men in the region who remained true to the Union throughout the war. As a reward for his loyalty, he was appointed to several commissions and committees that were instrumental in the development of Logan County. He eventually was elected as the first County Judge of Logan County. Mr. Ellington lived a long a fruitful life and passed away in 1890. He and many of his family are buried in Ellington Cemetery in Magazine.

Around the turn of the century, Millard reached its peak. The community contained a school house, a church, and various businesses but awaited only the Great Depression to scatter its inhabitants across the county.

Many of the prosperous Rogers family moved into the larger towns of Belleville and along what was to become highway 10. The price of farm crops bottomed out during the depression and residents joined the "Okies" and headed to California. Many sold their land to the government and large tracts reverted back into National Forest. Today, only a few stone foundations and a bridge across Shoal Creek remain to remind visitors of the town and people who lived in the region. The Rogers, the Ezell, and some of the Lee's are the only people who still own land and reside in the region.

Other small towns sprang up in similar places. Many of them were built on old traces and trails used by natives and, even earlier, served as game trails. Buffalo, native to Arkansas, would find the easiest and most assessable routes to grazing land, feeding higher up the mountain slopes in the hot summers and in the lowlands during the winter. Over a period of time, the trails deepened to form paths and then trails used by settlers. Highway 109 onto Magazine Mountain began in this manner. Areas having access to flat rich land and abundant water attracted settlers and these became the first communities. Corley, Chismville, Booneville, Shoal Creek and other communities began in this manner.

One of the oldest towns in western Arkansas, Booneville was founded about 1828, when Walter Cauthron built a log cabin and opened a store near the Petit Jean River in what was then Crawford County. According to the Cauthron family tradition, he intended to name the settlement Bonneville in honor of his friend Captain Benjamin Bonneville, an army officer stationed at Fort Smith, with whom he shared an interest in exploring Arkansas Territory. It is interesting in that Booneville was the first county seat but it was the county seat of Scott, not Logan County. When Logan County was formed in the

1870,s, Booneville was annexed to the Logan County and Paris was built as the county seat. Scott County seat became Waldron and Booneville was left out of the mix. The primary explanation was that the people in South Logan County favored the Confederacy.

Booneville, AR 1900

All Confederates that served during the war lost their vote for ten years. The Scotch-Irish individuals in the north part of the county were staunch unionists and, as a favor, were given the right to name the county and to locate the county seat, which they did, at Paris. The county was first named Sarber after a Yell County carpetbagger. In 1875, the former Confederates were once again allowed to vote and quickly changed the name to

Logan, a founding pioneer who lived near Chismville.

In 1828, the old Military Road was completed from Fort Gibson in Indian Territory to Little

185

Rock, Arkansas. This road became one of the major arteries connecting Arkansas with the East and several communities developed on this major line of transportation. The military were given $10,000 to construct the road and portions of it were contracted out to individuals living in the area. Section 16 was contracted by Henry Stinnett and sections 17-20 were assigned to Thomas Hixson. Stinnett either had a rougher tract of land than Hixson or was better at bargaining. He received $40 per mile or $200 for his section while Hixson received on $35 dollars per mile. The road was required to be fifty foot in width and have trees cut to the level of eighteen inches or so which was required height for wagons to pass over without catching. Bridges were extra expense and $300 was allocated for the bridge at Short Mountain creek but there were good crossings at Little and Big Shoal Creek and a passable one at Six-mile creek.

Community trading centers developed along the road, usually one about every six miles along the section lines. Even today, traveling from Fort Smith, the remnants of these small communities exist at this interval with Bloomer, Charleston, Branch, Caulksville, Paris, Subiaco, Midway, New Blaine, and Delaware at nearly exact six mile intervals. On the south side of the county, a road was constructed that connected Fort Smith to Markham Street in Little Rock by passing through Greenwood, Booneville, Magazine, Danville, Perryville, and through the mountains to the Capitol.

Stage routes developed along these routes, carrying passengers and mail overland. The famous Butterfield Stage was completed in 1858 and carried mail and passenger more than two-thousand miles across the country in

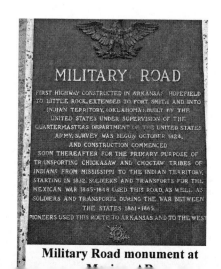

Military Road monument at

186

just twenty-four days. The passenger fair was $200. On its westward maiden journey, one of the passengers was a *New York Herald* special correspondent named Waterman Ormsby, who reported his travels in a series of articles. Travelers were in motion day and night, stopping only for meals and to switch out stock or equipment. On approaching a station, the conductor would blow a horn so fresh mules or horses would be ready and waiting.

One route ran from Illinois through Fayetteville, Arkansas and then into Fort Smith. On Second Street in Fort Smith, a line running from Memphis would connect with the northern line. This route from Memphis passed through the Arkansas River Valley with stops at Conway, Morrilton, Potts Tavern, Dardanelle, Stinnetts Station (Delaware), Speilerville (Osage Station), Paris (Moffat's Station), Charleston, Lavaca, and then into Fort Smith.

Ormsby reported,*" I had thought before we reached this point the rough roads of Missouri and Arkansas could not be equaled; but here Arkansas fairly beats itself. I might say our road was steep, rugged, jagged, rough and mountainous—and then wish for some more expressive words in the language. Had not Mr. Crocker provided a most extraordinary team, I doubt whether we should have been able to cross in less than two days. The wiry, light, little animals tugged and pulled as if they would tear themselves to pieces, and our heavy wagon bounded along the crags as if it would be shaken in pieces every minute, and ourselves disemboweled on the spot."*

Ormsby continued, *"The mules reared, pitched, twisted, whirled, wheeled, ran, stood still, and cut up all sorts of capers."* Sometimes fearing for his life, he would get off the wagon and walk. On one occasion, he was very glad he did, for the harness soon became tangled, the wagon wrecked, and the two lead mules escaped. The wagon driver disentangled the harness and

Fort Chadbourne Museum, Butterfield stage

continued the trip with only two mules. Against his better judgment, Ormsby got back on the wagon, although he wrote that *"if I had any property I certainly should have made a hasty will."*

Speilerville Mercantile, turn of 20th century

Many of the towns that developed in the Arkansas River Valley developed along these old frontier roads. Those include the string of towns along highway 65 north of the Arkansas River, and in 1926, along highway 22 which was built parallel but about a mile to the south of the Old Military road. Many communities literally moved the entire community to the south to accommodate the new road. Others such as Spieilerville, Ellsworth, Shoal Creek, and St. Louis Valley were bypassed and the communities died. Shoal Creek, located on the Military Road, had been a thriving community for many years. In 1900, it had three mercantile stores, a blacksmith shop, Methodist church, post-office and a mill. In 1904, a group of wildcatters decided to drill a 750 ft. oil well on Henry Anhalt's farm near the town. At about 500 feet, they hit a twenty-foot thick layer of sandstone and then a thick layer of coal. Gas, perhaps from the coal layer, blew out the well with a gusher of mud and water. Water continued to run from the hole after the rig was extracted.

Artesian Well, Shoal Creek

At first, a strong odor was emitted by the well and gas bubbles formed at its surface. The gas would burn, indicating it was probably methane from the coal. Eventually, the water cleared and a pipe allowing water flow was stuck into the opening. For years, area residents would gather at the well for parties, family reunions, and church events. Young men and women of the region gathered there to court and many bottles of moonshine and watermelons were cooled within the water. A vault, supposedly from a failed bank robbery, was left on the site and is used as a basin to catch water.

The well is still there; the water has flowed continuously for over one-hundred years. Shoal Creek Community is no-more. Highway 22, built one-mile to the south, absorbed all the area traffic and the area population followed, building homes along the new route.

Only a few miles of railroad existed in Arkansas prior to the Civil War. As soon as the war ended, railroad construction began in earnest across the U.S. Railroads received sections of land along the route they constructed. Sale of this land increased profits for the company in two ways. First was the direct infusion of money from the sale of the land, usually at a rate of a few dollars per acre in the less desirable mountains of Arkansas. The second profit resulted from those settlers using the railroad to transport themselves and their goods across the country. A rail road was quickly built from Little Rock, up highway 10, through Blue Mountain, Magazine, and Booneville. Another line ran along the western border of the state passing through Fort Smith and southward into Texas.

In 1890, Paris was a prosperous town of about 800 people. It contained nine general stores, a bottling company, two newspapers including the Paris Express, and Paris Academy.

Coal, discovered in the Arkansas River Valley prior to the Civil War, became a valuable commodity. Mines were established at Greenwood, Hartford, Hackett, and throughout Johnson County. The appetite for the fuel was insatiable and, when larger coal mines started opening in Logan County, the Arkansas Central Railroad decided to build a rail system to Paris.

First Train to Paris, March, 31, 1899

The railroad was completed in March of 1899 and the first train arrived to much fanfare.

Scranton, Arkansas, named after the famous Pennsylvania coal and iron fields, started

developing its coal fields during this same period of time and a thriving community developed there as well. From 1917 to 1957, thirty-one privately owned coal mines operated in the Paris area, employing about 2,000 miners. At the height of the industry,

Subiaco AR. Train Station

Paris shipped an average of 250 to 300 tons of coal daily. One year, more than 13,000

railroad cars of coal were shipped from the Paris mines. Many families moved to Paris to

191

take advantage of the employment opportunities and good wages of the coal mines. At a time when other areas were struggling economically, business activity in Paris flourished as a result of the thriving mining industry. The mining industry continued until the 1950s, when the demand for coal decreased.

Subiaco, established as a Catholic Monastery and academy, received land grants from the railroads to aide in the establishment of a strong German Catholic farm community that contributed to the success of the railroad. Cotton, vegetables, and livestock produced by

Coles Drug and Logan County Bank; early 1900's, Historical Society Photo.

these thriving families contributed much to the community. More than anything else, the development of the automobile changed the culture and face of Arkansas. Once isolated, now people had access to the rest of the world. In the 1800,s, travel of just a few miles required hours of time over bumpy and dusty roads while being pulled by recalcitrant and obstinate animals. Conducting major business or governmental enterprises such as buying property, paying taxes, or even purchasing goods often required overnight travel. Many counties including Logan, Franklin, Sebastian, and others created two county seats to lessen travel.

Railroads cut down that time and expense but were available in select locations. People living in the delta rode the train to Blue Mountain or Magazine, exited to face a several hour trip by carriage up to the hotels on Magazine Mountain. Only the wealthy could afford these long and expensive vacations that allowed escape from the heat and miasma of the lowlands.

Automobiles and the modern highway changed that. Highways 65 and 22 were major routes for truckers carrying supplies across the country and road stops developed at regular intervals to care for them. Products they carried became readily available to the general public and changed what we ate, how we dressed, and even our opinion of the outside world. Hilltop Café, between Paris and Subiaco, offered a resting place for the drivers as well as food and entertainment in the form of pin-ball games. Similar places sprang up across the U.S., often accompanied by motel rooms and service stations.

Large groups of people suddenly had the ability to move great distances with relative ease. When the depression hit, many of them did just that, joining the Okies on their way to California and places west.

One of the more interesting stories of towns occurred during this period of time. As highway 22 was being constructed, several individuals began to acquire property and buildings at intersections along the road. Twelve miles east of Paris, the confluence of highway 22 and highway 109 began to attract farmers and businessmen who wanted close to the highway. Many, including the Parson, Whites, and Trusty's moved from the surrounding valleys and hollows and built homes in the community. The local Assembly of God church moved from Sorghum Hollow road and constructed a new building along the highway. Three stores were soon constructed and Mrs. Nancy King, according to the Paris Express newspaper, was in the process of building a roadhouse. The latter was reported as a matter of pride which indicates the term roadhouse had a quite different connotation at that time. In the 1920's, a roadhouse would be somewhat akin to what we know as a truckers plaza and gas station; a place to refuel, rest, and get food.

Midway store in 1950's

Obviously, without general approval, several of the residents decided that the enterprising community was large enough to receive a name. Noting that large pumpkins grew throughout the area, the name of Pumpkin Center was chosen for this new metropolis. Though a source of pride for some, others in the community felt the name reflected a country bumpkin image- one the clearly did not want to be associated with.

A humorist by the name of Cal Stewart had created the mythical New England town of *Punkin Center* and had made a career of deriding the simple people who lived in the town. It was clear that this name would not suffice for such an up and coming community. Jessie Parson, one of the leaders in the area, had been in Mississippi hunting when the name was selected. Immediately upon his return, he and others organized a community meeting to discuss the problem. After debate, the name of Midway was

selected. According to Dr. J.N. Pennington of the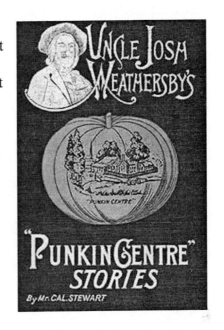
Paris Express, Midway was the ideal name. It might
one day become the hub of the universe, located as it
was midway between Paris and London, just down
the road from Dublin and New Blaine, and half-way
between Magazine and the Boston Mountains. The
name continues, the community has shrank to just a
church, car lot, community building, and a few
homes.

Each small community was centered on a church and school house. Often these building
were one and the same with daily school sessions followed by church on the weekends.
Initially, schools in Arkansas were only for the wealthy and larger communities. Planters
and others with money often sent their children out of state for an education. After the
Homestead Act and other legislation were enacted to disperse of the vast federal lands
owned by the United States after the Louisiana Purchase, the 16th section of each
township was reserved for education. The land was often sold and the money used to
build a small school. With land selling at two-dollars or less per acre, the few thousand
dollars obtained was not enough to provide adequate funding. Called "blab" schools, the
school often consisted of one school room and one teacher who taught multiple grades up
to year eight. The students recited or "blabbed" their lessons out loud at the same time so
that the teacher could ensure they were studying.

By 1874, the state mandated free basic education for every child but funding to support

this education was never established. Teachers pay was low and was often paid from community collections set up for school support. In 1903,

New Blaine School building, 1952

the average teacher salary was only $33 per month.

By 1900, about two-thirds of white students were receiving some sort of education. In contrast, only two per-cent of black students in the state were being educated and those were in schools segregated by race. Students often attended sporadically with sessions built around agriculture farming cycles.

During this time, small schools dotted the country-side. In the early 1940's, Arkansas had 1,589 school districts. Small schools existed at Mt. Salem, Rich Mountain, Ione, New Blaine, Shoal Creek, Branch, and other small communities. By 1957, consolidation of districts left many of the old buildings deserted.

Academies could be found in the larger towns. Academies offered students the opportunity to continue their education in a campus environment and for a fee.

Clarence Davis Photo, Paris Academy, 1909

Paris Academy, built in 1885 at a cost of $12,000 was one of 26 accredited by the University of Arkansas. Students could attend four months tuition free but had to pay from one dollar and fifty cent-four dollars a month for the other five months of school. Room and board cost an additional eight dollars a month. Some parents traded fire wood, labor, and food for tuition- this at a time when pork was selling for five-cents a pound. In 1909, the Academy moved from the site where Paris Mercy hospital now stands and built a new academy on 10th street at a cost of thirty thousand dollars. Paris elementary was established in the old academy. Both buildings saw continuous use until the 1960's when the elementary school burned and the present day middle school was built to house grades 7-12.

Today, Logan County has five school districts, Johnson and Franklin counties have four each.

As year went by, gravel roads turned into highways, then super highways, and finally interstates opening up a new world and new opportunities. Small schools were consolidated into districts, churches grew too small to support a pastor, industry took the place agriculture, and machinery took the place of farm labor.

Little did people of the time know that the automobile and roads that attracted them and caused the development of their community would soon serve as the same conduit elsewhere for their children and grandchildren. Better jobs and wages beckoned from Dallas, St. Louis, and even Los Angeles and the small towns and communities shrank and many disappeared.

Main Street in Magazine, 1918

It is a continuing problem, one now faced by many rural areas across America. Where do we go from here? How do we maintain our country heritage and way of life in a face paced world? Is our region destined to be Millard's or is there a strong enough appeal to continue to live and raise families in the *Shadow of the Mountain*?

Men and Women of Integrity

The Arkansas River Valley is composed of some of the most beautiful and complex landscapes in the world. Along the rivers and streams are the deep rich black soils and flat lands that make up some of best farm lands on earth. Its area encompasses mountain slopes covered by pine and hardwoods, rolling hills suitable for livestock, and plenty of natural resources. Colorful rainbow hued rock and mossy sandstone provide building materials sold across the county and natural gas and oil reserves exist across the region yet, the single most important factor that makes a location what it is, is the people. Although the River Valley has produced a few people of national and world renown, what the area holds in abundance is the hard-working common person who is the backbone of America. Synonyms of integrity are honesty, probity, rectitude, good character, principle, ethics, righteousness, morality, virtue, fairness, truthfulness, trustworthiness, and honor. These people might not make earthshaking decisions every morning on things that affect the lives of millions, but they show up at their jobs, take care of their families, lead moral lives, and serve as examples of what makes this country great. This is the story of some of the best of the best.

Runaway Pig

The Scrudder family was of Dutch descent. After migrating to the America, the family had settled in Eastern Tennessee and then, during the mid- eighteen hundreds, migrated

to Arkansas. A century later, families of that name were scattered throughout the region with a number of them living in and around the Midway community. Dow and his wife Ilene bought one of the stores in Midway and, when it burned, moved the business across the road in a sandstone building on the corner of highway 22 and 109. Dow drove a Paris school bus, helped with the store, and spent as much time fishing as possible. The bus route started at David (Man) Millers home in Sorghum Hollow where he picked up all the boys and Donna and extended to Midway and then up the Military Road to Subiaco. His load of sixty or so students were a contentious lot consisting of family groups of Miller's, Horn's, Varnell's, Trusty's, and Rhineheart's from the Midway community plus the Catholic families of Strobel's, Huber's, and McCombs from Subiaco.

Place that many kids on a bus for an hour and a half trip each way and your assured that domestic tranquility will not long prevail. Mornings were usually pretty peaceful. The bus route began before seven so most of the load was half-asleep until arrival in Paris. The afternoon journey was not nearly as quiet and much more eventful. Packed from front to back with many standing, the bus would lurch down the road, kids talking and arguing at the top of their lungs. It was hot, it was loud, and dust would roll into the windows every time the bus slowed or stopped. Squabbles would break out between those wanting the windows up or down, who would sit with who, who said what about whom, and various other items of world-shaking importance. Dow was a patient man; sundry events such as verbal altercations, brother and sister tussles, and an occasional book lost out the window were relatively inconsequential and would generally be settled between those involved. When a disagreement became serious enough to result in loss of teeth, limb, or life, he would interject himself into the argument. Riding a bus was regarded a privilege, not a right and, when warranted, bus drivers has more weapons on hand to combat the evils of adolescences.

200

One particularly hot afternoon, the bus had no more than escaped the Paris city limits when one of the many Horn prodigies received his first warning for pushing an elementary student out of the seat. This was followed quickly by two or three more glares in the rearview mirror, a violent thump on the brake when the miscreant was hiking down the bus aisle to the backseat, and finally to pulling the bus over and stopping on the side of the road. Realizing that something serious and more exciting than the norm was about to occur, the bus quieted to a roar and then to absolute silence.

We had just turned onto Carter Lane at Subiaco, six miles from the Horn residence. Dow turned around in the seat, calmly opened the door, and motioned for the young offender. "Guess this is where your trip ends for today," he stated motioning for the kid to exit. Defiantly, the boy jumped out of the bus, glaring at the driver. Just as Dow closed the door, the older sister jumped up, "You can't throw him off the bus." Dow opened the door back up and motioned for her to join her brother. Two other familial members joined in the entourage, leaving only the youngest of the family on the bus.

The small group of offenders stood desolately in the center of the road facing a long walk home. The bus door closed and down the road we departed, gleefully waving goodbye to the offenders,

Parents can sometimes be the worst of nightmares for teachers or bus drivers. Too a devoted parent, their child is the angel and, contrary to any evidence presented, are the victims in any incident in which they are involved. One such little demon existed on our route. He was constantly badgering younger kids, irritating the others, and being a general pest and nuisance. After enough violations to fill up a small book, the older students retaliated by making him the brunt of their pranks. His socks were removed and deposited out the window, he was awarded noogies and wedgies and various other cruel and unusual but well deserved punishments. Rather than preventing his misbehavior, his actions escalated. In addition, to elicit sympathy, he reported every event that happened, and many that did not, to his mother. Being the dutiful parent that she was, she took out her considerable ire upon the poor bus driver by waiting at the bus stop with little Junior and berating poor Dow constantly, loudly, and consistently. We actually began to feel sorry for him. As we approached the stop, mom could be seen standing beside the road with the little devil. Since it was early in the morning, she would still be in her gingham nightgown, often with a bonnet on her head, house shoes flopping on her feet, and a flushed, angry look on her face. We sat and enjoyed the spectacle, knowing what was going to happen. Opening the door set off the initial volley of insults whose volume and range was directly proportional to the amount of time the door was open- and Junior would take his time getting on. The mother was livid, nearly incoherent she was so mad, and all of here energy was focused on the driver, not on the real culprits sitting in the back grinning and enjoying the show. Dow would try to calm her and to explain what was happening, all to no avail. Finally the door would close, down the road we would go, leaving her in swirls of dust and debris

planning her next morning visit with Dow. No wonder Dow liked fishing so well. It had to be a great reprieve from putting up with us five days a week.

The Scrudder store was utopia for the children of the community. During the 1960's, soda had doubled in price but still was a bargain at ten cents- especially if you purchased the large 16 oz. Pop Kola. Ilene would dip out one scoop of ice cream in a cone for a nickel or three for ten cents and they had a variety of flavors. Nothing like a dip each of butter pecan, chocolate, and cherry vanilla ice cream.

The same store sold groceries, gas, car parts, and animal feed so it was a one-stop mall for all the family needs. Paris was twelve miles away and travel there was for the weekends.

Solon and Edward Scrudder had grown up in the community, attended some church college, and then returned to Midway to farm. Hard-working religious men, they were pillars of the community and involved in every facet of church life at the local Assembly of God. Both were deacons in the church for extensive periods of time and Solon was Sunday school superintendent. He married Avelene Bingaman of Ellsworth community. She was an extraordinary lady in every way. The daughter of a circuit riding Cumberland Presbyterian minister, she and Solon made a perfect couple. She worked on the farm, taught Sunday school, and sang in the ladies quartet.

Both were tall, lean, and spare in appearance. Solon, like all the Scrudder men, was strong featured with dark hair and prominent nose and ears. Generally he was very serious in nature; saying what needed to be said in a slow, measured, well-thought out manner.

Avelene was freckled, light-complexioned, blue-eyed, with a head covered in bright orange-red hair. When she was outside, she blistered easily so she often wore a sunbonnet to protect herself. Raised as a preacher's kid, she had a host of funny stories she recited as life-lessons when teaching our Sunday school class. Even today, I shudder when I forget and utter some slang word such as dad gum, shoot, or even worse, dang it.

These were vile obscenities when Avelene was growing up and uttering them would get your mouth cleaned using ole Dan's left over corn cobs. Ole Dan was obviously the Reverend Bingaman's toothless old horse that would gum, roll, and slobber all over the corn while partaking of his meal. Avelene would vividly describe the spectacle of yellow and green juice dripping on the cobs as Mr. Bingaman threatened to clean vile mouths and tongues with the left-over's from ole Dan's meal. She would laugh, shake her finger emphatically in front of her face and, with her high pitched voice, admonish us to watch our P's and Q's, a memory that remains in my mind till today.

Mr. Bingaman must have believed strongly in object lessons. Avelene's younger brother often served as the focal point of her illustrated lessons. The child must have been a true horror to rear because he was constantly in trouble, especially for his behavior during church service while his dad was occupied. He was known to crawl under the pews, tie knots in little girl's hair, and generally squirm and make noise during the service.

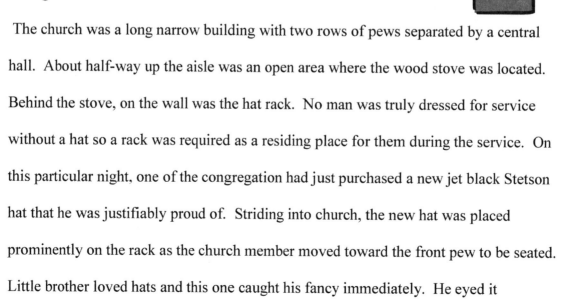

 The church was a long narrow building with two rows of pews separated by a central hall. About half-way up the aisle was an open area where the wood stove was located. Behind the stove, on the wall was the hat rack. No man was truly dressed for service without a hat so a rack was required as a residing place for them during the service. On this particular night, one of the congregation had just purchased a new jet black Stetson hat that he was justifiably proud of. Striding into church, the new hat was placed prominently on the rack as the church member moved toward the front pew to be seated. Little brother loved hats and this one caught his fancy immediately. He eyed it throughout the song service, crept up closer to the rack during testimony's, and, overcome by desire during the preaching, he stood up on the back of the pew and removed the hat. Avelene looked on in horror as he dropped the new hat onto and over his head. It was large, falling down to his shoulders, and completely blocking out the service. Alarmed at the sudden darkness, he miss-stepped as he turned, and immediately thumped headfirst onto the floor. Realizing his error in judgment, he crawled rapidly toward the rear of the church, squashed stetson still covering his head, with anxious owner chasing behind trying desperately to recover his hat. Church service ended quickly that Sunday.

Reverend Bingaman was silent on the way home in the wagon. Arriving in the barn, he retrieved the culprit from the wagon seat. Mom, sensing that trouble was about to erupt and that punishment was on the way, headed to the safety of the kitchen. Avelene, totally devoted to both father and little brother, sat torn between fleeing and watching what was to occur. "When men do things they are not supposed to, they are punished," sternly stated the reverend. "When they continue doing evil, the punishment becomes worse." Do you know what they do to those that are really bad? "Spank them," stated little brother, fully expecting belting on his backside. "I mean when they are really bad and people have tried everything else," stated the reverend. " Nooo Sir," quivered little brother, now very concerned with what was about to occur.

"They hang em," stated the reverend, grabbing a thick hemp rope that lay across the stall and slinging it over the rafter above. "Please, dad, don't, don't hurt him," pleaded Avelene, anticipating the rapid demise of her only sibling. Tears rolled down her face as she got between her dad and brother. Reaching around her, Mr. Bingaman grasped the boy and tied the rope tightly around the middle of his son. Brother burst into tears and immediately began to plead his case, promising to never, never, ever be the cause of future problems. Quickly, Mr. Bingaman yanked on the rope, pulling the little monster off his feet and into the air. Little brother let out a startled bleat and began to swing around the room, zooming first in one direction and then another. Quickly, fright changed to childhood amazement at flying and he began to place his arms out to his side, slicing through the air with the ease of the new-fangled airplanes that he had heard about. Reverend Bingaman's stern face changed and a smile crossed his face as he yanked the flying child up and down and round and round. "Rooooom, rooooom," laughed the child, excitedly flapping his arms and going in circles around the room. Soon, all three were sitting on the floor, tears running from their eyes, laughing until their sides hurt. " Guess that's enough punishment for today," stated the reverend as he placed his arms around both children, " time to get into the house."

Solon and Avelene lived in a small white house on the old Military road, about a mile west of Midway. The land was rolling hillside covered equally by grass, rock, and trees. Solon was assistant manager at the Paris Oklahoma Tire and Supply Company (OTASCO) in Paris and subsidized their livelihood by gardening and raising livestock. Everyone in the community raised pigs- usually having an enclosed wooden pen a good distance behind, and hopefully downwind, of their home. The pig pens were messy affairs, filled with knee deep mud, excrement, and water. Families kept slop buckets in their house, into which they dumped left-over food, potato peelings, and other materials we now deposit down our disposals. This material was general mixed with chops (cracked corn) and shorts (wheat hulls and mixed grain) and feed to the hogs each day.

Despite their looks and habits, pigs are actually quite intelligent. They could anticipate

feeding time and would begin to fidget around the pen, standing on their hind feet and

snorting as they heard the backdoor opened at feeding time.

On this particular spring afternoon, Solon was on his tractor,

working the garden just north of the pig pen when Avelene

exited the backdoor, carrying the five gallon bucket of slops to

their several pigs. With bonnet covering her head and long

gingham dress flapping around her ankles, she was greeted by

wild snorts and bellows from the pigs anticipating the arrival of supper. The largest of

the pigs, an ornery three hundred pounder called Red, repeatedly lunged at the side of the

pen as Avelene duck walked across the backyard with her head down watching slop pour

over the sides while slinging the heavy bucket between her legs.

With a loud crash, the top rail of the pen collapsed. Immediately, Red demonstrated an

athletic ability only before seen in the white-tail deer of the region, leaping the fence and

aiming himself straight at the slop bucket dangling directly in front of Avelene. Solon

looked up from his plowing just in time to alert his wife to the impending disaster.

"Head him off, Head him off," he screamed, hoping against hope that his skinny wife

could stop the oncoming porkster. Avelene's head popped up, saw Red bearing down on

her, and hearing Solon's admonition, put down the bucket. Stepping in front of the

bucket, she spread her legs and flapped her gingham dress. "Shew, Get back into pen,"

she screamed, bending her body at an impossible angle and flapping her dress briskly.

Not to be deterred, the pig ran straight for the bucket, now located directly behind

Avelene's billowing skirt. She could later describe the mean pink eyes, the determined look, and the amazing speed of Red in the seconds before he plowed directly into her. The speed of the animal lifted her off her feet and threw her up over the shoulders of the animal. Startled, she grasped for a handhold and ended up locking both arms around those large future hams. Her legs locked, holding her firmly facing rearward on the running beast. Red, with head now covered by dress, an unknown screaming object on his back, and in total darkness due to both eyes being completely covered by clothing, increased his speed, heading east.

Solon sat on the tractor, spellbound by the spectacle before him. Red picked up speed as he headed down the incline, grunting with the exertion. "Whoa, whoa," screeched Avelene, bouncing up and down and side to side on the critter.

Avelene and Solon Scrudder

Red quickly determined he was a sprinter rather than distance runner. His three hundred or more pounds began to slow and make a large circle back in the direction from whence he had come. As he ran back up the slope, Avelene's long legs began to settle lower and lower around his neck. Finally, exhausted he slowed to a crawl and Avelene's toes came in contact with the slope.

Feeling the safety of the hillside, she released her death grip on the shank of Red and sprawled onto the ground. Red ran back to the pen, jumped the fence, and submerged himself back in the mud. Avelene just lay there; splattered with dark smelly pig mud, dress askew, bonnet twisted over one eye and half of her face. Solon still sat watching from the seat of the tractor. Finally, Avelene got up, swaying on her feet, a glare on her face. "That pig took me to Midway and you just sit there and watched," she was so mad she was stomping her feet. Solon just sat there, a small smile finally crossed his face, and then a larger smile, and suddenly a deep chuckle that became a roar as it burst from his lips. "Humpf, humpf," bleated Avelene, placing her hands on her hips and stomping her feet. Solon reached into his rear pocket for his handkerchief and began wiping his eyes, his entire body racked with laughter. "Humpf, Humpf," emitted Avalene, headed back to the safety of her kitchen. She couldn't decide if she was angry with Red for taking her on the ride or for her normally placid husband finding it so entertaining.

The Backwoodsman

William James was the oldest of the ten sons of Nettie and Lee Varnell. William was

always skinny as a rail, stood 6 foot 7 inches tall, and was tough as nails. William, as the oldest, absorbed tremendous responsibility when his father, Lee, died at an early age. With nine other brothers, he and the family traveled across the country working as migrant farmers in Arkansas, Arizona, and California.

Willam and Dorothy Varnell   Although he had limited education, he was always self-sufficient and could do anything he wished to try. Most of his adulthood, he suffered from severe ulcers that caused him to vomit blood and required trips to the emergency room for temporary care. Refusing any charity or government assistance, he was always out of the hospital in a day or two and back at work logging or working in the rock quarry, living on Alka-Seltzer and coffee. From childhood, he was a hunter, often killing rabbits with rocks. Later in life, his home was packed with various guns, ammunition, and traps. Every day possible, he was in the forest searching for game, trapping for fur, or merely exploring.

William lived about a quarter of a mile west of highway 109 on Swartz rock quarry road. Purchasing a few acres of land, he soon constructed a rough pine home, a barn, and several outbuildings. He plowed his garden with plow and mule, raised vegetables, cut his own wood for cooking and heat, and generally lived off the land. Memories include going over to his home in the winter and him having a roaring fire built in the living room stove. The stove was more of a kitchen stove with pot lids on top. Usually a pot of coffee sat slowly heating on the stove. William would get out the poker and push the wood back and forth, sparks soaring across the room. Soon the fire would be roaring and the metal on the side of the stove would glow cherry red from the heat. William would have his shoes off and his stocking feet up on the metal hearth heating.

Dorothy (Crow) Varnell was always reading- most of the time Zane Grey westerns if she could get them- her thick black hair hanging in stiff braids down her back. She always had club feet and a difficult time in getting around but William was always there to help. It was amazing how tender and easy he could be with her and they took care of each other right up until the end. One of the hardest days he had in life was when she passed away and he was too ill to go to the funeral- he just sat there and rubbed the tears in his eyes when the family tried to share pictures from the funeral. A few weeks later, he was also gone to be with her.

My first experience trying to ride a horse was at his home. William loaded Sonya, Ray Neal, and Roy Lee Varnell onto his old donkey only to have the ever active Ray pulled the hair on the animals back. Normally docile, the critter went straight up and then took off like a rocket spilling kids topsy-turvy in all directions. Sonya landed plush on her elbow, a large soft flesh balloon sticking up from arm. She survived but I wasn't sure the donkey was going to when William finally got him under control.

William knew where the fern covered caves were located, where waterfalls tumbled down the mountainside after exiting from the center of wagon wheels cut by settlers into the cliffs, and where Civil War deserters hung out to escape retribution. He knew the deepest swimming holes, the highest cliffs, the oldest roads, and who had lived along those roads in days long since gone. A wealth of knowledge in ways of surviving in the harsh days of the dust bowl and depression, he would have been a leader during the days of the Old West and the frontier.

Hard to provoke but even harder to control when irritated, he was a man to be reckoned with. He always ran a string of traps, selling the fur and eating the game that he collected. In his later years, he was running his traps near Sand Ridge and found several traps missing. He began looking for them and ran across the county work crew gathered near an old bridge on one of the nearby lanes. William asked them about his traps. One of the younger men finally responded, acting put off and angry by the question, "I just took your trap off a dog that got caught in the danged thing."

William explained to him that he was sorry that a dog had been trapped but, being on Swartz property, the dog was where he shouldn't be. In return, the county worker gave him a lecture about the evils of trapping. William finally had enough, "My traps are legal, now, you can go get me my trap." Putting on a show for the other workers, the young man looked at William and mockingly replied, "Old man, I threw that trap down there in the creek. If you want it, why, I guess you'll just have to swim out there and find it for yourself." The men sitting around joined him in laughter at the skinny old man. William said not a word, just turned and walked off with the laughter ringing in his ears. Heading to his car, he retrieved his 12 gauge from the rack and returned to the party. Returning to the bridge, he looked more like Buford Pusser from *Walking Tall* than the harmless old man from moments past.

"I asked you very nicely to return my trap. I paid good money for that trap and I intend to have it back," he said in a quiet but level voice. The men were no longer laughing; they were looking at the young trap thief warning him to do as told. The young man got up quickly, heading to the creek as fast as he could move. William looked at the other men, "I think the boy needs some help." That's all the conversation that was needed. Within minutes, the entire group was beating through the grass and shallow water at the edge of the creek. Retrieving his trap, William headed back to this pickup and home.

Like most of the Varnell's, he had a deep sense of humor and laughter. Working with a construction crew building a house for Dow Scrudder, he was given the task of pushing wheelbarrows of stone for the rock layers. Steady but slowly, he pushed load after load up the hill and over to the wall of the house and deposited the rock. Exasperated at his work speed, the foreman approached him. "William, is that the only speed you have?" he inquired, glaring at his worker. William slowly set down the wheelbarrow, seated himself on the stone, and began wrapping himself a cigarette made of Prince Albert tobacco.

"No, he replied, but I think you'll like it better than my other speeds." The conversation ended with that remark and the foreman stomping off in frustration.

It was common for the men around Midway to meet around the stove in the back of  Woodard Mosley's store. They would pull up chairs or sit on the ends of coke crates and watch the big pot-bellied coal stove while sharing the daily gossip and tall tales. William happened to stop in while the men were discussing their failed attempts at catching a huge bass in a local pond. Each man recited his failed attempt with the stories growing consistently with each repeat. Obviously, the bass had eluded capture and had torn off hook after hook and lure after lure. William sat down with his ever present cup of coffee and listened earnestly as each man recited his efforts. Finally, without the hint of a smile on his face, he tilted his cap back and firmly stated, "Well, you guys can stop wasting your time on that fish. I caught him last week when I was down there fishing." The men were dubious about his claims. "Nobody can catch that fish, he is just too old and wise to fall for any trick you could come up with," one argued. "Nope, I caught him," William patiently explained. "How do you know it was the fish we're talking about?" explained another. "Had to be," William exclaimed with a gleam in his eye as he got up and walked away, "he had so many of your hooks in him I sold him for junk iron."

As he got older, he lost his teeth but hated to wear dentures. While on a trip to Shreveport to check on a family member, he and my parents stopped for lunch at a roadside dinner. Always having a sweet tooth, he ordered a piece of coconut pie from the pie safe. The waiter placed the pie slice, already on a paper plate, on a dish and served it to William.

After consuming most of the pie, William commented, "You know, that pie is really good but the crust is harder than heck." Mom checked out the pie and began laughing, "William, you just ate half of a paper plate." This without the benefit of his dentures!!!

The Preacher

In 1942, a new pastor was elected at Midway Assembly of God. Little did he or the

Gorman and Imogene Daniel, 1940

congregation realize that he would be there raising a family and serving as pastor for most of the next forty-three years. With his steady demeanor, quite authority, wisdom, and white flowing hair, Reverend Daniels always looked and acted the part of the minister- kind of like a local Billy Graham. Like Rev. Graham, he was respected, not only by his congregation, but by everyone who came into contact with him. In an age marked by ministerial failures, he was a steady rock of faith and stability.

Totaling more than sixty years in the ministry, he was district presbyter for several years and served as Executive Presbyter for the Assembly of God for fourteen years.

In the 1980's, he and Bobby Johnson of Van Buren journeyed to Honduras for teen missionary trips. For weeks, he agonized about he and his wife taking their first airplane trip only to find out that they thoroughly

Rev. Gorman and Imogene Daniel

214

enjoyed the that part of the journey. Busses in Honduras were another matter completely.

No stop lights, narrow winding lanes, and breakneck travel were the rule of the day.

Teens on the trip reported his complexion as ash white when he got on board and, within

a few minutes he was busy praying for deliverance and for the bus driver's soul.

One inflexible member of the church constantly led the congregation in singing the same

song every service. Begged to get her to offer more of a repertoire, Brother Daniel

proved his wisdom by simply cutting that page out of all the song books on stage.

Devoid of the music, the congregation received a change in venue the following week.

A congregation is much like a classroom. There is always about a dozen things going on

at once. One night pastor paused for a dramatic moment during the conclusion of his

sermon. Immediately, a scratching noise resounded throughout the building. Looking

around the sound could be traced to the elderly Roscoe Griffin who sat on the outer

portion of the front row. Uncomfortable with his new dentures, he had his pocket knife

out busily reshaping them to fit his mouth. On another occasion, my sister Glenda sat on

the end of the pew. At five years of age, she just could not keep her eyes open for the

entire service. The pastor concluded the sermon, said the final prayer, just started to say

amen, when Ker plunk, Glenda upended off the end of the slat bench and landed on her

head on the floor. "Ten seconds too long a sermon," exclaimed Bro. Daniel as he

dismissed us.

For all of his duties and responsibilities, he was far from reserved and unapproachable.

For forty years, he christened us when we were born, prayed for us when sick, joined us

when we married, laughed with us when we laughed, cried when we cried, and was there

with us when we laid our loved ones to rest.

Another outstanding man and minister is Abbot Jerome Kodell, OSB of Subiaco Abbey.

Friar Jerome resigned as Abbot in 2015 after twenty-five years leadership of the

Benedictine monks at the Abbey. Prior to his election as

abbot, he taught at the Abbey's academy and served as the

formation director for young monks. Fr. Jerome is nationally

known for his efforts in promoting Bible study among

Catholics. He founded the popular Little Rock Scripture

Study program and is the author of the bestselling Catholic

Bible Study Handbook as well as other books. Locally, he is

Friar Jerome Kodell, OSB

known for his ecumenical work throughout the River Valley. He has been actively

involved in the Logan County Ministerial Alliance hosted, as well as attended, various

Protestant services as part of community worship.

While Abbot, he worked closely with area business, civic groups, and industry to

encourage the economic viability and growth of the region. He is and was actively

involved in community affairs and encouraged both the Abbey and the Academy to be

actively involved in events throughout the region. Promoting Christian cooperation and

alliance, rather than bitterness and division, has been his gift throughout his ministry.

The Teacher

The 1950's brought some exceptional young teachers to the region. In the mid-fifties,

Guy Fenter joined the staff at Paris Schools as a coach and English instructor. He was

soon joined by Marlon Davis, Charles Harris, and Bentley Allen- all young, unmarried

men that roomed together during their first years of teaching. Fortunately, they all soon

found that Paris was not only a good teaching location, but produced some of the prettiest and smartest young ladies to be found. All married local girls and remained in the region for the remainder of their careers.

Guy Fenter was assistant coach for the 1956 undefeated Eagles, coach for the girls' basketball team, as well as a teacher. He soon moved to Charleston where he served as superintendent of schools for a number of years before starting becoming the director of the educational cooperative at Branch that is now named after him.

The chain gang: Marlon Davis, Bentley Allen, Charles Harris

Charles Harris taught math at Paris for several years, became principal, then assistant superintendent before succeeding Guy Fenter as Charleston superintendent. Marlon Davis changed careers and served as educational book representative and salesman before retiring.

Bentley Allen was, is, and will always be known for being the consummate classroom teacher. For more than thirty years, he demanded the best from the math students he taught at Paris Schools. Graduates will attest to his classroom skills and many will attribute their success in life to lessons he taught in his classroom, the athletic fields, and in Paris Boys and Girls club. All of them may not remember the algebra; they will remember his work ethic, his integrity, and his sense of humor.

Although only about five and a half-foot tall, Bentley was a very athletic guy. Cousin to professional baseball player, Don Kessenger, Bentley loved baseball and almost any other athletic activity. He coached several sports and assisted the athletic department in every possible way, including keeping statistics and running the chains. Along with

Mickey Patterson, he coached several seventh grade football teams to undefeated seasons. More importantly, he imparted some life skills that shaped young men and women's lives.

By the 1970's, education had drastically changed. Early education was marked by large classes, exacting lessons in the three "Rs," and extremely strict discipline meted out with frequent paddlings. On one occasion in the late 1960's, Danny Varnell had journeyed downtown to Raney Drug during lunch and purchased a bottle of pure cinnamon. It was common for students to soak toothpicks in the bottle to produce a fiery-hot candy. It was more of a mark of manhood than enjoyment to extract and suck on the toothpicks. Placing the small bottle in his pocket, he forgot to completely tighten the lid. Halfway through Coach Stephens's science class, the liquid began to drain from the bottle, through his pants pocket, and onto his thigh. Wrenching back and forth in pain but too fearful of the teacher to ask to leave class, he waited until the bell, ran to the gym and into the shower, only to discover a large patch of his hide was no longer present. On another occasion, a young lady intimidated by her teacher, wet her pants because she didn't want to ask to leave the room. Bentley never was too concerned with trends, the newest pedagogy, or the latest item to come through the Department of Education. He simply knew his students and he knew how to teach.

Mr. Allen loved his graph board. About four feet square, it was made of wood and covered with green cork and hung on the west wall of his room. During class, he would use a long wooden cue stick to point out coordinates on the board.

After a particularly trying lesson, Bentley was emphasizing major points by jabbing the stick at various points on the board. The board was rocking back and forth off the concrete wall that held it and the wire holding it in place became more and more loose. "Mr. Allen," one of the girls stated, raising her hand. "Just be quite and listen a minute," stated the teacher. "But Mr. Allen," interjected another student." Turning to face the students, an irritated Mr. Allen firmly stated, " The reason you didn't get this the first time was you weren't listening." "Now pay attention and let me show you again. This Y coordinate will intersect about right"- and at this point Mr. Allen jabbed the board once last time. Completely free of the screw holding it in place, the board tumbled forward striking the teacher firmly on the back of the head and shoulders and knocking him flat to the floor. Bentley looked up into the blue eyes of the girl helping to remove the board from his back, "Mr. Allen, I was trying to tell you that board was coming off the wall." During the 60's, Paris elementary school burned, a new high and elementary school were constructed, and a whole new crop of teachers were hired. These included Charles Douglas, Gary Garner, Mick and Judy Patterson, Elgenia Williams, Bill Wright, James and Linda Simon, Elwood Brooks, Joyce Hander, and Bill Vanmeter. Mr. Allen, Coach Jim Clay, James Morris, Mrs. Long, and a few others had an entirely different crew to work and contend with. These became the core to one of the finest groups of people and teachers ever collected in one district. Although having a great sense of humor, Bentley was a little on the type A personality side and more than a little nervous and jumpy; a fact that other teachers, especially Bill Vanmeter, loved to use against him. Discovering that Bentley used an electric eraser cleaner to remove all the chalk from his board cleaners, Bill determined to have some fun at Bentley's expense. The electric eraser cleaner worked much like a vacuum cleaner. The teacher would insert the eraser into rollers which would extract the chalk and then blow it into a bag where it was stored until it was

219

filled. Waiting until Mr. Allen was out of the classroom, Bill slipped in and unbuttoned three of the four buttons that held the bag in place. Waiting until half-way through the next class, Bill sent a student into Mr. Allen's room with some of his erasers he wanted clean. Anyone working with

Electric Eraser Cleaner

Mr. Allen knew he hated having his class time disrupted. Shaking his head and fuming, he muttered to himself all the way to the back of the room where the machine was stored. Irritated, he reached down and flipped the button. Immediately, a white cloud of chalk enveloped the room. Ghostlike students began to clean the white powder out of hair and eyes. Grabbing up the machine and yanking the wire from the wall, Bentley fumbled his way to the second floor classroom door and gave it a pitch. The machine hit the grass near the concrete eagle located in the student courtyard below, much to the enjoyment of Vanmeter and his students who were laughing and applauding Mr. Allen's reaction. Red in the face, Bentley glared at the group who laughed even harder. Finally, joining in the laughter himself, he returned to his classroom. The machine remained in the courtyard for the remainder of the day.

Mr. Allen would often go over the lesson, make an assignment, and then would play the radio while students worked. He would always tune into KCCL, 1490, " *The Country Sounds of the River Valley"* which was the local Paris station. The station, owned and operated by the Hixson family, played country music, presented local weather, advertisements, and local sports. The announcer, along with many of the locals, loved to meet at the 22 Café owned by Mayor Cecil Patterson and have coffee. Bentley was a

friend of most of the group- a group that loved playing practical jokes. Bentley turned the radio on in class only to hear his name. "Mr. Bentley Allen, local school teacher, has recently taken on a second job. He is now the area distributor of *Grit* newspapers. Now, we all need to help Mr. Allen out by going down to the 22 Café to purchase your newspaper for the low, low price of fifteen cents. Hurry on down," implored the announcer. Kids giggled, Mr. Allen turned red and immediately headed to the office. Calling the announcer, he questioned what was going on. "Just repeating the request that was on my desk when I arrived this morning," explained the

announcer. "I want it off there," ordered the teacher. "No problem, Mr. Allen, I take care of that right now," replied the announcer. Mr. Allen returned to the class just in time to hear, "Well guys, just heard from Mr. Bentley Allen. His new shipment of *Grit* has just arrived and you need to rush right on down and get your copy." Speechless, Mr. Allen turned off the radio. *GRIT* was a weekly newspaper sold by kids and was somewhat akin to the tabloid news of today.

For months, Cecil Patterson had a stack of the newspapers available at the 22 Café with a deposit box available for Mr. Allen.

The Paris Boys and Girls club celebrated fifty years of service in 2014. Bentley Allen, more than any other person, helped to get the Paris Boys club started. He helped get the Fair Board to allow use of their building as a meeting place and eventually oversaw the transition of the club to the present site at the Old

Bentley Allen, 1950's

Paris Armory. He served as first director of the club and often his responsibilities included delivering kids home, paying for expenses out of his own pocket, and babysitting kids without parental supervision. He oversaw the establishment of youth ball fields, organization of peewee football, and eventually, to the addition of girls as part of the club. The most amazing part of the story is that the Allen family has two girls and no sons.

The Allen's exemplify what is good, clean, and wholesome about rural communities. A close family, he, his wife, and two girls could be seen riding bikes around town and doing things as a family. They were active in church and community and gave of themselves to others. Mr. Allen and his wife work at the Community Service center on a regular basis, dedicate time to Logan County retired teachers, and Mr. Allen can be seen many afternoons at the Paris Boys and Girls Club still tutoring math to kids of the community.

Joyce Hander was an exceptional science teacher; more importantly she was an exceptional person and friend. Under her tutelage, Paris was able to boast of having five students in medical school at one time, an exceptional accomplishment since the school admits only fifty students per year. Nurses, physical therapists, x-ray technicians, and other care providers abound as graduates of Logan County schools. Many of these students got their start in her biology and chemistry classes. Many of her students visited her home and were treated to home cooked Tex-Mex food and entertained by Dr. Hander, who was president of the school board, and by the Hander family. She was also very active in Girl Scouts as a regional director and inspired girls to be involved in the sciences. In her early fifties, she planned to retire and she and Dr. Hander were going to serve as missionaries and provide veterinary assistance and teaching to underdeveloped countries. This was not to be. Joyce became afflicted by cancer and was forced to undergo chemotherapy. With no substitute

Joyce Hander

available and with students that needed to get a solid science education, she placed an old wig on her now bald head, braced herself into her chair and withstood the pain as cancer afflicted her spine and back, and taught until no longer able to stand. Students at Paris High need to know the reason the science wing is known as the Joyce Hander addition.

Irben and Mary (Parson) White came from a long line of Arkansas pioneers. Both the White and Parson families migrated into the region from Tennessee and settled in the hollows of Magazine Mountain. The Whites settled in the Mt. Salem community, where they farmed, worked in timber, and raised livestock. During the Civil War, most of

Irben and Mary White

the family members remained loyal to the Union, often at great risk and cost to the families.

Irben eventually moved to Sand Ridge on highway 22 and managed his own business which included trucking, farming, and managing a rock quarry business. The land he owned produced some of the best watermelons in Arkansas. Irben's specialty was the yellow-meated watermelons, so dark they were nearly orange in color. Always trusting of his neighbors and customers that happened down the highway, he would leave melons and money beside the highway unattended. People would figure their bill from the weight written on the melon and leave the money in the cigar box. In all the years he sold melons, he stated he never lost a dime. "If they stole any money," he once stated, "it is ok, they probably needed it more than me."

A member of Midway Assembly of God, he attended youth services up until he was eighty years old. Secretly, he purchased a piano for the youth hall, bought van gas for youth trips, and often paid for every child tickets to Magic Springs, Silver Dollar City, or water parks.

In his later life, he loved to give away knives and handed out over seven-hundred to friends, neighbors, and visitors.

One of the most inspiring men of my educational career is Garvin Green. He was my high school counselor and later, was editor of the *Paris Express*. He was a native of Magazine and grew up exploring the hills and hollows around his home. After years in military service and completion of college, he served as teacher and counselor at Paris and Magazine schools. He was also a minister in the Primitive Baptist Church, a man of many talents and much wisdom. His tireless effort kept the dream of Magazine Mountain Park and Lodge alive and without him, it would just be a grown over jungle. During his earlier years, he collected volumes of material about the history of Magazine Mountain and compiled only a small piece into his book.

Later, while I was teaching, he and I trekked around the mountain and he pointed out many of the places and recited many of the stories that you hear in this volume. He was

always a great inspiration to me and one of the reasons I choose a career in teaching. A trail, a bluff, a building on Magazine- something should be named for this man who contributed so much to preserve the history of the mountain where he grew up.

Garvin Green

Coaches

For years, the word Coach in North Logan County meant one man, Big Jim "Eagle" Clay.

A solid rock of a man, Coach Clay exemplified the image of a football coach. Standing

on the sidelines puffing his pipe, his calm demeanor and carriage contrasted greatly with

all too much of what goes on in sports today. With over two-hundred victories, he was a

winner on and off the field.

In the early 1970's, he took his football team across the state to the playoffs. Many

schools had just undergone integration and some communities remained segregated.

After arriving at a restaurant, all the students and coaches were seated and served except

for the black athletes. Noting the lack of

service, Coach Clay approached the

owner and was told that the restaurant

would not serve black students. Coach

Clay immediately notified his assistants to

get the students up and prepare to go

elsewhere. Either all would be served or

the restaurant would get no Eagle

business. The owner quickly changed his

mind and all were served.

Paris played the Alma Airedales, Van

Buren Pointers, and other large schools as a part of the 4-A conference. While playing in

the first quarter against Alma, the Airedale's lined up to kick a long field goal. The ball sailed to the right, hit about the five-yard line, and bounced through the end zone. Three points, indicated the officials. Immediately, Coach called them over to the side and began to politely question the officials. Players and fans could see that the conversation was becoming more and more animated. Coach finally pulled off his cap, stomped his feet, threw his cap onto the ground, and stomped it several times- all to no avail. The Paris crowd was dumbstruck!!!! This was Coach Clay!!!! With grim and determined faces and with a fired up crowd behind them, Paris delivered a sound thrashing to the favored Airedales.

Coach Clay eventually retired from teaching and served several terms as Mayor of Paris. Coach Dennis Crane served as an assistant to Jim Clay and eventually became head coach of the Eagles. Dennis was a California native and played college football at the University of Southern California with the national championship team that featured O.J. Simpson. Dennis eventually played several years of professional football for Atlanta Falcons, Washington Redskins, and others. Students would often bring him old football cards from the years he played in the NFL to autograph. After working as assistant coach at Arkansas Tech, he and his family moved to Paris. One of the most successful coaches at Paris, he lead the team to several state playoff berths and a one –time preseason number one ranking. Known as the gentile giant, he was a compassionate, caring Christian man who loved and cared for all students- not just the athletes. He served as Fellowship of

Dennis and daughter Dena

Christian Athletes director for several years. The entrance to Eagle stadium is named in his honor.

Businessmen

Hobbling up the street, weaving side to side on his damaged legs while pushing a heavily loaded cart of concessions, Gerald Baskins provided an inspiration to hundreds of kids as he went about his daily business. Stricken with disease at an early age, Gerald's body was bent and deformed by nature but his soul and spirit was unaffected. Living in an age in which a man could simply retire and draw disability while moping about fate, Gerald was an exception. He started his business selling

Gerald Baskin

concessions at the Logan County Courthouse and then gradually expanded his business by adding a cart which he loaded down with soda, chips, and candy. He could be seen

pushing the cart up highway 22, across to 10th street, and up to the ball fields each day during baseball season. It was a task!! His legs were bent and crippled and the exertion of pushing the cart would extract a toll on any man. The other local with such determination was Leroy McConnell. Leroy suffered from polio when he was about ten years old. He survived polio but spent over a year in an iron lung. When released from the hospital, he had to

228

relearn to walk on twisted and deformed legs. He was fitted to leg braces that twisted his

legs back into semi-normal shape and given shoes to adjust his height and gait.

Genetically, he should have been a large man but the disease made him a foot shorter and

a hundred pounds lighter than his brothers.

He realized early on that he could not make a living working in the timber or as an

Leroy McConnell
Social Studies

industrial employee so he devoted himself to his studies. At

Arkansas Tech University, you could hear him dragging his

legs and heaving himself up the stairs to class.

At class, he excelled and eventually was hired by

Superintendent Bob Ehren at Paris where he taught social

studies. Before the days of teaching student involvement,

Leroy would have the kids scattered all over the classroom

drawing maps, working in groups, and doing reports. Teaching is just now catching up to

his pedagogy.

Leroy had a dry sense of humor and was always telling jokes, often on himself. Once, he

told the story that he had three grown men down on the ground begging him at the same

time. When questioned, he stated they were on their knees saying, "Leroy, you come out

from under that car and we are going to beat you to death."

Both of these men did not choose the easy way. Grit, determination, hard work, and the

attitude that they would make the best of what life offered sets these men apart. Both

were an inspiration to all who encountered them!

Pleasant, upbeat, positive, friendly are all words that describe Harold Rogers. Described

by many, including my father, as one of the best men they ever meet, Harold was a perfect salesman for Bob Roger Chevrolet. People from across the state would journey to Paris just to purchase a car from him because they knew he was honest, upfront, and a good Christian man.

Prior to selling cars, he had a successful dry cleaning business. He was always good at working with people who instinctively sensed his honesty and friendliness.

A life-long member of Paris First Assembly of God, he was one of the first to organize the older members and get them to go on trips and outings. The group would go to Muskogee to see the azaleas, to Fort Smith to eat, Eureka Springs for entertainment, and just meet to talk and share. He always enjoyed collecting and restoring old cars and enjoyed taking them to car shows around the country. On his to-do list was to go the entire length of old highway 66 from Chicago to California in vintage automobiles.

When people talk about him, they always use the sentence, "He was a good man." What better way to be remembered!

On Sunday mornings, his deep, sonorous voice could be heard throughout the Gray Rock community as he expounded upon the word of God. Rolling across the flat bottom land, his bass tones resonated with the congregation who joined with him in worship. The Gray Rock church really just got going about the time church services concluded in Paris. Worship usually consisted of warming up for an hour or so with Sunday school, congregational singing, special songs, and testimonies and then letting Brother Logan preach till he got tired. As he warmed up, he would take his suit coat off, wipe his glistening face with the handkerchief from his back pocket, and exhort the crowd to live

in a manner pleasing to God. Accompanied by amen's, hallelujah's, and hand-clapping,

he delivered the word of God to his congregation.

Born in Logan County in 1906, he was eventually able to acquire several acres of prime

farm land near Cotton Town and produced some of the best cotton crops in the region.

An August 17, 1954 *Paris Express* photo shows him and Mayor Guy Conley at the Conley gin where Buford has just produced the first bale of cotton for the year. The week before, he had delivered a load of cotton to Dardanelle, the first bale produced in Yell County. At that

First Bale of Cotton of 1954

Reverand Buford Logan

time, he expected to produce a half-bale of cotton per acre on his farm. During the

1950's, he employed many area farm workers who helped weed the cotton in the spring

and harvest it in the fall.

As he grew older, in addition to preaching, he worked part-time at several jobs in Paris.

He ran his own business cleaning several stores including Dillon's grocery and

Warehouse Market after hours. He also assisted in running the produce market and other

general jobs around the store. Customers, both black and white, loved him and would

catch him the aisles to chat. Dennis Baltz of Warehouse Market enjoyed having him to work simply because he was the ideal greeter and brought in customers who enjoyed visiting with him.

He was a very jumpy person. Employees loved to slip up behind him and "goose" him in the ribs. In his seventies, he would still jump straight into the air and oomph in his loud voice. Good natured, he would smile from ear to ear, "I'm a gonna watch out for you son," he would state with a big smile, "can't let you be slipping up on me like that." Buford Logan was an esteemed man of God and did much to bridge the gap between the black and white communities of the region. His bright smile would light up his entire face and he beamed with the joys of life. With his warm heart, positive attitude, and sense of humor, he influenced generations.

Everyone in South Logan County fished with Jack Hatcher. Growing up in the "bottoms", he knew every honey hole and private pond in the region. Fishing was a passion with Jack, one he practiced at every opportunity. On his lunch break at the local grocery stores, he would often take his rod and reel and fish at the Legion Hut. At his funeral, the pastor asked every person who had ever fished with Jack to stand. More than half of the nearly three hundred people present stood to their feet. Jack spent a lifetime as butcher in various grocery stores in Paris. During the 1960's, he was butcher at Nation Wide grocery on highway 22. He later worked for Dennis Baltz at Warehouse Market and Town and Country Market.

The Hatcher family came from a long line of athletic baseball players. Jack's father Harold and Uncle Jim both played with the old coal mining baseball teams that toured the country playing baseball. Both Jack's brother Bill and cousin James later were good enough to play for various college or traveling teams and the entire family was and is still active coaching various little league and boys club teams.

Working in the grocery business, Jack knew everyone in town and loved to play pranks on many of them. A part of the crew that meet for coffee at 22 café as well as at Harold Dorrough's barbershop at noon, there were few events that occurred within the region that he wasn't involved in. One of the local characters was Woodrow Lowrey. Woodrow was built somewhat like the Max truck bulldog that adorned the hood of his truck. A former truck driver with a gruff, boisterous voice, he would stomp into Cecil's 22 with his old hat jammed down over his receding hair, chewing on the end of an unlit cigar, and looking for someone to pester. Dennis Baltz, owner of Warehouse Market grocery, was his favorite target and he made life miserable for Dennis by spitting paper wads into his water, moving his chair when he attempted to sit down, or simply charging his breakfast to Dennis's account. As a loyal employee, Jack determined to help Dennis get even. One fall morning, Woodrow stomped into the café late, threw his old beat up cowboy hat down on the floor beside his table, and sat down. He proceeded to loudly order his breakfast and pick on the morning crew. Seeing the old hat laying upside down on the floor, Jack quickly handed Dennis

Jack and Betty Hatcher

the jar of syrup and pointed at Woodrow's hat. Catching on, Dennis deposited about half the jar into the upright hat.

Running late, Woodrow finished his coffee and, like always, reached down, grabbed up his old hat and smashed it down on his head. Immediately the sugary, torrid, brown mass slid down his face and hung in strands off his chin. Tendrils of the sticky mixture dripped from the cigar stub and gripped every whisker on his inflamed face. Grabbing a napkin, he tried to wipe the goo only to have it smear in large lateral streaks, now interlaced with the disintegrating paper from the napkin. Leaping from his chair, he exited the café, followed by howls of laughter from the morning crowd.

On another occasion, Jack was involved with the crew that placed a clear plastic broken glass decal over the front window of a friend's car while the fellow was enjoying breakfast. Complete with a rock laid on the hood, the realistic setup appeared to be the result of recent vandalism. Leaving the café, the young

man discovered the damage his vehicle had incurred. Rushing back into the café, he explained what had happened. Everyone in the store encouraged him to immediately call the Sherriff who would track down and

arrest the culprit- that is everyone except one of the men who slipped out of the café to remove stone and decal. Within minutes, police showed up at the door. "Someone threw a rock through the window of my new car," exclaimed the young man. "Done it while I was having breakfast; just totally ruined my new car." "Had a rash of that happening," exclaimed the policeman, "Come on out and I'll write up the report." The entire crowd followed the pair out of the café. The young man was talking excitedly, explaining his case to the policeman. Pointing out his car, he excitedly began to point out the damage while walking closer and closer to the car. "Broke my window into a thousand pieces-threw a rock right throu....," the stopped in mid-sentence as the noted his undamaged window. Totally confused, he began, "it was broken, just a minute ago it was broke with a rock on my hood." The Sherriff, in on the conspiracy, solemnly began to berate the young man. "Son, you ever heard about false reports?" he asked, winking at the crowd. "You could get into some serious trouble calling me off my duties like this."

"But I'm a telling the truth," the young man choked out. "I'm telling you it was broke."

"Did any of you men see this broken window," questioned the Sherriff. To a man, the group replied to the negative, shaking their heads and looking at the now very chagrined young man like he was bereft of his senses. "I am going to let you off on this one," stated the Sheriff, walking over to his car and turning the lights off. "It just better not happen agin!"

Profusely thanking the Sheriff, the young fellow exited the parking lot while the entire crew rolled on the ground with laughter.

Paris is a typical Arkansas small town with lots of good, solid hard-working Christian people who find humor and laughter a good cure for all ailments. Jack fit right in with these folk!

Ed Williams, H.S. Photo

D.J. George of Booneville, Alfred Gordon of Magazine, Frank Ahne of Scranton, Frank Willems of Subiaco, Joyce Fiddle, Gene Davis and Ed Williams of Paris are typical of many of these people. Proud of their home towns and wanting them to prosper, these men give invaluable time and expertise in making things happen. A life-long resident of the county, Ed Williams ran his own wrecker and repair shop for years and is one of the most well-thought of men in the region. Since youth, he has been involved in virtually every civic organization and program designed to promote the area. He grew a beard and dressed western for Frontier Days, one mounted a motorcycle in a gorilla  suit and smoked a cigar while riding in the county fair parade, and reconstructed old automobiles that were shown all over the South. For several years, he has clung to the side and top of the Logan County courthouse and placed the annual Christmas light display that draws hundreds of spectators into the county. He and Gene Davis worked on the Paris Eiffel Tower that has recently been placed on the square, an unexpected tourist attraction that has already served as a wedding site, reception area, and a place where tourist love to make selfies.

Mr. George is the face of Booneville football and assists in every aspect of the game, a full-time job in a town where the successful football program takes up twelve months a year. Mr. Gordon is the author of *King of the Mountain*, a book that describes his life and a huge amount of the history of Magazine. Frank Willems was a one of a kind. A successful farmer, he took his expertise to Little Rock and served as state representative for many years. Among his many accomplishments, along with Lloyd George of Danville and Garvin Green of Magazine, was the restoration of Mt. Magazine lodge and park. Joyce Friddle has been so active in preserving the history and culture of the region; it would be hard to describe all of her achievements. The Logan County miners museum is just one of her many projects.

No story would be complete without including my friend James Simon. A native of Mississippi, James taught in several locations before he and wife, Linda (Crawford) Simon returned to her home town of Paris. James served as principal of Scranton schools for a period of time before joining the staff at Paris High school teaching algebra and math.

James was a unique individual in that he could change from the serious Type A math persona to the type Z wild, gregarious, most-fun loving, out-going guys you could meet and he could do this within a matter of minutes. Excitable, once when the tornado warning went off at school, he forgot where the kids were to go from his upstairs classroom. With the buzzer screaming in their ears, the kids asked where to report. "Go, just go," gestured the flustered teacher with his arms circling in every direction. The students left like a covey of quail, mixing with classes from throughout the building.

So absorbed in teaching, he would wipe the board with his shirt sleeves and step into the trash can while circling his desk, James would expound on math, school, and life. For years, he could be seen driving around town in his old blue pinto car with his pet dog hanging out the window eating snicker bars. James described his car maintenance program by saying his car had gone two-hundred thousand miles without a change of spark plugs or a change of oil and cleaned only when he left the windows open during a rain. While licensing his new car, he was asked by the assessor what he planned to do with his old ford. "Give it to you," replied Simon, handing her the keys and walking off. Her son drove it for several more years.

During the faculty fishing trips, Simon could survive most of the week without sleep, often keeping everyone else up with his antics ranging from personnel firework demonstrations to playing drums with big pots and pans. Attempting to get even, the men stuffed his suitcase his suitcase with red teddy's and ladies bikini underwear from the local Walmart, hoping to get him into hot water when he got home. Unpacking his suitcase, Linda extracted and displayed them to Simon. Unperturbed, Simon explained, "Took a lot of my time to go select those for you." Linda wasn't concerned anyway; she knew James to be solid, reliable, and hard-working and she also knew the people he worked with!

According to some, life is like a great flowing stream and we are but bits and pieces of flotsam and jetsam. We have little choice and are just carried along for the ride. I like to think that some individuals are rocks in that stream. The rock stands firm! When hit with turmoil, it remains and the stream is diverted and changed. I like to think of these people as rocks in the stream. They have changed the path of all around them.

There are many, many individuals that are deserving of recognition. Many go unnoticed and without thanks but these people, not the politicians, not the media stars, not the celebrities or those of national import are the ones that make America great.

Bibliography

Alvarez, H. G., 1983, Fire in the Hole, *South Sebastian County Historical Society*, 1983, 195 pp.

_____, Ancestry.com. *Arkansas, Confederate Pension Records, 1891-1935*. "Parker, William C. #24606", Provo, UT, USA: Ancestry.com Operations, Inc., 2011.

Assenmacher, Hugh, OSB. *A Place Called Subiaco: A History of the Benedictine Monks in Arkansas*. Little Rock: Rose Publishing Company, 1977.

_____, *Biographical and Historical Memoirs of Northwest Arkansas: Benton, Carroll, Crawford, Franklin, Madison, Sebastian, and Washington Counties*, Goodspeed Publishing Company, Chicago, 1889, 1382 pp.

Bolden, Ben, "Civil War: Fort Smith Forces Began Organizing To Fight" *The Times Record*, Sunday, May 1, 2011.

Bolton, S. Charles, *Remote and Restless: Arkansas 1800-1860*, The University of Arkansas Press, Fayetteville, 1998.

Campbell, Thomas H., et al. *Arkansas Cumberland Presbyterians 1812–1984: A People of Faith*. Memphis: Frontier Press, 1985.

Carter, Joe and June Carter. "Union Church and School," *Logan County Historical Society: Wagon Wheels*. "Union Church and School," Fall/Winter 2001, Volume 21, No. 2.

Carter, June, "The Mad Stone," Wagon Wheels, *The Logan County Historical Society*, October, 1980, pp. 62-65.

Chism, Ben B. "Letter to Mrs. Harlow Bishop, Junction City, Texas, from Paris, Ark., May 28, 1895", *Arkansas in the Civil War Message Board*, Posted by Kenneth Byrd on 10 February 2007, 3:23 pm, Accessed 2 August 2011, http://history-sites.com/cgi-bin/bbs53x/arcwmb/webbbs_config.pl?noframes;read=14728

Chandler, Angela, *Guidebook for Petit Jean and Mount Magazine Geological Tour*, Arkansas Geological Survey, Sept. 24-26, 2007.

Chowdhury, Maria, Midwives, *The Encyclopedia of Arkansas History and Culture*, http://www.encyclopediaofarkansas.net/encyclopedia/entry-detail.aspx?entryID=3781, accessed 12/5/2013.

Christ, Mark ed., 1994. *Rugged and Sublime; The Civil War in Arkansas*, The University of Arkansas Press, Fayetteville, 207 p.

Cox, David, A History of the Battle of Devil's Backbone, Arkansas, *Explore Southern History .com*, http://www.exploresouthernhistory.com/DevilsBackbone2.html , accessed March,16, 2014.

Dane, Nancy., *Tattered Glory: A Documentary Civil War History of the Arkansas River Valley,* N.p.: 2005.

Davis, Paul; Kenrick, Paul, Fossil Plants. Washington, DC: Smithsonian Books, 2004. ISBN 1-58834-181-X

DeBlack, Thomas, Civil War and Reconstruction, *The Encyclopedia of Arkansas History and Culture,* http://www.encyclopediaofarkansas.net/encyclopedia/entry-detail.aspx?entryID=388 , accessed Aug. 6, 2014

DeBlack, Thomas A., *With Fire and Sword: Arkansas, 1861–1874.* Fayetteville: University of Arkansas Press, 2003.

Dodds, Gilbert F., Camp Chase: The Story of a Civil War Post, *Franklin County Historical Society,* Columbus, OH, 1961.

Dunham, J.S., editor, Jail Escape, *The Van Buren Press*, Van Buren, Arkansas, May 9, 1871.

Edwards, John Newman, *Shelby and his Men, or The War in the West*, Waverly, MO: General Joseph Shelby Memorial Fund, 1993.

Ferguson, R., The Henry Wood Ferguson Family of Ferguson Valley, http://records.ancestry.com/Henry_Wood_Ferguson_records.ashx?pid=44517623, accessed March 16, 2014.

Fletcher, Sonya P., The Last Public Hanging In Arkansas, *High Points in the History of Logan County*, 1964.

Ford, Salem H., *Reminiscences of S.H. Ford, Captain of Company "F", 2nd Reg. - General Jos. O. Shelby's Brigade of Missouri Confederate Cavalry - 1861-1865,* The State Historical Society of Missouri, http://shs.umsystem.edu/index.shtml, accessed 2/27/2014.

Foreman, Grant, The California Overland Mail Route Through Oklahoma, *Chronicles of Oklahoma,* Volume 9, No. 3, September, 1931. http://digital.library.okstate.edu/Chronicles/v009/v009p300.html accessed 3/1/2015.
Gabbert, Jim, "Resettlement Administration," *Encyclopedia of Oklahoma History and Culture*, http://digital.library.okstate.edu/encyclopedia/entries/R/RE032.html, accessed 12/28 2013.
Getler,W and Brewer, B, Rebel Gold: *One Man's Quest to Crack the Code Behind the Secret Treasure of the Confederacy,* New York: Simon & Schuster, 2004.
Gorden, Alfred, *King of the Ozarks, Mount Magazine,* Self-Published, 1999, 406 p.
Green, Garvin, Footing it on Mount Magazine; Mill Pond, *Paris Express-Progress*, Paris, AR, Thursday, December 11, 1980.
Green, G. and Simon, Don, *Mount Magazine, A History*, Paris Express-Progress, 2004, 127 p.
Hanley, Ray and Hanley, Steven, *Remembering Arkansas Confederates and the 1911 Little Rock Veterans Reunion,* Arcadia Publishing, San Francisco, CA, 2006.
Hawkins, Van, Cotton Industry, The Encyclopedia of Arkansas History and Culture, http://www.encyclopediaofarkansas.net/encyclopedia/entry-detail.aspx?entryID=388 , accessed Aug. 6, 2014.

Hempstead, Fay, *A Pictorial History of Arkansas From Earliest Times to the Year of 1890*,
St. Louis and New York, N.D. Thomson Publishing Co. 1890.

Hill, Luther, *The History of Oklahoma*, Vol. 2, The Lewis Publishing Company, Chicago, 1910, p. 291-292.

Huff, Leo. "Guerrillas, Jayhawkers and Bushwhackers in Northern Arkansas during the Civil War." *Arkansas Historical Quarterly* 24 (Summer 1965): 127–148.

Johnson, James, Arkansas Reports: Cases Determined in the Supreme Court of the State of Arkansas from March, 1914, to April 1914, Arkansas reports, Vol. 112, Arkansas Democrat Press, 1915.

Kennedy, Steele, *A Spanish Galleon in Arkansas*, **http://okietreasurehunter.blogspot.com/2009/06/spanish-galleon-in-arkansas.html**, accessed Feb. 24, 2015.

Lasater, Burel, Personnel letter to the Pension Commissioner, Shoal Creek, Arkansas, Feb. 15, 1886.

Mackey, Robert, *The Uncivil War, Irregular Warfare in the Upper South*, 1861-1865, University of Oklahoma Press, 2004.

McRae, Dandridge. "Dandridge McRae Papers". *Muster roll, Captain John R. Titsworth's Company, Third Regiment, Arkansas Infantry Volunteers (organized in Franklin County, 1861 June)*. Arkansas History Commission. Retrieved April 5, 2011.

Monaghan, Jay, *Civil War on the Western Border, 1854-1865*, University of Nebraska Press, Lincoln and London, 1955.

____, Montgomery County: Our Heritage, *"They Can't Go Home,"* Vol. 1, Page 340.

Nuttall, Thomas, *A Journal of Travel into Arkansas Territory during the Year 1819*, University of Arkansas Press, Fayetteville, 1999.

Ormsby, Waterman L. *Butterfield Overland Mail*. San Marino, CA: Huntington Library Press, 1988.

Owen, David Dale, SHORT MOUNTAIN FROM THE HAGUEWOOD PRAIRIE SANDSTONES, SHALES AND THIN COAL OF THE MILLSTONE GRIT, *Second Report of a Geological Reconnoissance of the Middle and Southern Counties of Arkansas, Made During the Years 1859 and 1860,* C. Sherman & Son, Printers, Philadelphia, 1860.

_____. *Outlaw Murrell: An account of his Capture near Florence, his Imprisonment, Death and Mutilation,* Florence (Al.) Times, Saturday, Feb. 28, 1895, p. 1.

Parler, Mary Celestia, ed.,"Folk Beliefs from Arkansas; Death and Funereal Customs, Collected by University Students." Vol. 8. 1962. Special Collections. University of Arkansas Libraries, Fayetteville, Arkansas.

Payne, Betty, and Oscar Payne. *Dwight, A Brief History of Old Dwight Cherokee Mission 1820–1953.* Tulsa: Dwight Presbyterian Mission, 1954.

Rafferty, Milton, ed. *Rude Pursuits and Rugged Peaks: Schoolcraft's Ozark Journal 1818–1819.* Fayetteville: University of Arkansas Press, 1996.

Rajakumar, K (2000). "Pellagra in the United States: A Historical Perspective". *Southern Medical Journal* **98** (3): 272–277. ISSN 0038-43.

Rohrbach, Jill. *"High Point of Arkansas Continues to Lure Pleasure Seekers,"* Arkansas Department of Parks and Tourism, 1999.

Roster of the 11th Wisconsin Infantry, Co. G, The "Randall Zouaves" http://11wisconsinregiment.soldierstudies.org/?p=13 assessed Nov. 27, 2013
_____ , Roster of Confederate Soldiers of Georgia, 1861-1865, Volume 4, Longino & Porter, Hapeville, Georgia, pages 249-340, 1959.
Shirley, Glenn. *Belle Starr and Her Times: The Literature, the Facts and the Legends.* Norman: University of Oklahoma Press, 1982
Scott, Kim, The Civil War in a Bottle: Battle at Fayetteville, Arkansas, *The Arkansas Historical Quarterly,* Arkansas Historical Association, Publisher, Vol. 54, No. 3 (Autumn, 1995), pp. 239-268.

Scott, Mark. *The Fifth Season: General "Jo" Shelby and the Great Raid of 1863.* Independence, MO: Two Trails Publishing, 2001.

Sizemore, Ted, Sunrise Service on Mount Magazine, *Paris Express*, April 26, 1954.
Steele, P. & Cottrell, S., Civil War in the Ozarks, Pelican Publishing Company, Louisiana, 2003.
Sutherland, Daniel E. "Guerrillas: The Real War in Arkansas." *Arkansas Historical Quarterly* 52 (Autumn 1993): 257–286.

Sutherland, Daniel ed. Guerrillas, Unionists, and Violence on the Confederate Home Front, University of Arkansas Press, Fayetteville, 1999.

_____, "The Brave Arkansians," The New Era, Fort Smith, Arkansas, September 30, 1863.

Trusty, Gordon, Personnel Interview, Midway, Arkansas, June 29, 2014.

_____, "Prospect of the Farmers-Bushwhacking," <u>The New Era</u>, Fort Smith, November 14, 1863.

_____,"The Civil War in Logan County." *Wagon Wheels* 1 (Summer 1981): 18–38.

_____, *"Wild Bill" Heffington*, Arkansas State Gazette, Little Rock, June 13,1863.

The War of the Rebellion: A Compilation of the Official Records of the Union and Confederate Armies. Series 1, Vol. 22, Parts 1 and 2. Washington DC: Government Printing Office, 1888.p

The War of the Rebellion: A Compilation of the Official Records of the Union and Confederate Armies. Series 1, Vol. 41. Washington DC: Government Printing Office, 1893.

Elizabeth Titsworth., *Paris: One Hundred Years* (Paris, AR: Paris Chamber of Commerce, 1979), 9-10, 12-14.

Barry Vann, "Irish Protestants and the Creation of the Bible Belt", *Journal of Transatlantic Studies,* 2007 5(1): 87-106.

Webb, James, *Born Fighting: How the Scots-Irish Shaped America,* Broadway Books, U.S.A, 2004.

Wehner, Christopher, 2008, The 11th Wisconsin in the Civil War: A Regimental History, McFarland and Company, Publishers, 237 pp.

White, Irban, Personnel Interview, Sand Ridge Community, Aug. 1996.

Whayne, Jeannie, "Early Twentieth Century, 1901 through 1940," *The Encyclopedia of Arkansas History and Culture,* http://www.encyclopediaofarkansas.net/encyclopedia/entry-detail.aspx?entryID=3781, accessed 12/ 5/2013.

Wing, Tom, ed., A Rough Introduction to This Sunny Land: The Civil War Diary of Private Henry A. Strong, Co. K, Twelfth Kansas Infantry, Butler Center for Arkansas Studies, 2006.

"Wild Bill" Heffington ," Arkansas Gazette, Little Rock, June 13, 1863.

Wilson, Bill, Bushwhacker Bill Wilson Rides Again, Revelade Publishing, 2012.

Young, Bennet H., *Confederate Wizards of the Saddle*, Nashville, TN: J.S. Sanders and Company, 1914.